DRIFTWOOD PRESS

EDITORS

CREDITS

Independently published by *Driftwood Press*
in the United States of America.

Fonts: Satellite, Garamond, Cinzel, League Gothic,
& Merriweather.
Cover Image & Content Illustrations: Coz Frimpong
Cover Design: Sally Franckowiak
Magazine Design: James McNulty

Published in January 2020
ISSN Print: 2578-7195
ISSN Online: 2331-7132
ISBN-13: 978-1-949065-05-3

Please visit our website at www.driftwoodpress.net
or email us at editor@driftwoodpress.net.

ISSUE 7.1

Table of

Contents

The Smile Contest

Alan Sincic

The children gathered along the back wall of Miss Connor's class in a line that would have been—were it not for the cracks in the blue linoleum floor—perfectly straight. One crack in particular stirred in Farrel a desire.

It looked like a volcanic ridge from out the bed of an ocean. Into the crevasse where the tile pooched upward he thrust the tip of a sneaker. Wriggled the foot. Crowbarred at the broken flooring. The white rubber cap of the shoe—already loosened to a hinge from a season of play—peeled off completely. Scalped. He kicked at the shred of white. Strike one. Kicked again. It pogo-ed off down the aisle between the tiny desks.

"Farrel?" Miss Connor always sang, not the name of the child, but the syllables that made the name, as if the name were the opening bar to a melody she'd been trying, for the life of her, to remember. "Are you one of my Old Faithfuls?"

"Yes, ma'am."

"You are?"

"Yes, ma'am."

"Then who was that Silly Willy I just saw from out the corner of my eye?"

"I don't know, ma'am. It weren't me."

"Glad to hear it. Then would you be so kind as to fetch that little scrap of something or other I just saw from out the other corner of my eye?"

"Yes, ma'am."

And so he did.

"That was so gallant of you," said Miss Connor as she fingered the scrap of rubber. She smiled. "It would be so nice if you could do me one more thing."

Farrel nodded. *Gallant.* He didn't know what it meant exactly—something about brave—but it burned in a gentle way. If you could slip on a skin made out of cinnamon, that's what it would feel like. A cinnamon skin.

"If you could be the line-watcher, that would be so nice." Miss Connor pointed to the back of the line. The children snickered. "What we want," she said to the class in a melodious drawl, "is a line with no wrinkles."

A special line to match the special day. The apple of the earth all ruddy with the dawn. The birds piping and the crisp of the cloud and the chill breath of a moon over yonder in the dark. Today the day of the Smile Contest. The children felt the stir of something new from the moment the truck pulled into the lot beside the lunchroom. Like a mail-truck painted white, the big kind, you know, or like a Ice Cream wagon with the panel flanks and the bay in the back big enough to juggle puppies in.

The King of Ice Cream. That's the way Farrel pictured himself. Gliding, smooth as a bar of soap, between the green hills of Ohio and into the little towns like Smallville in the days of Superboy or whatever they called that neighborhood Dick and Jane and Sally and Spot in the reader all rambled around in. *Run, Spot, Run!* He would live in the truck, and in the white dungarees with the broad pockets and the white jacket and shirt and the silver change-maker strapped to the belly like a belt of ammo, and the children would all come running when he'd roll down the lane with a ring of the bell and a wave of the hand but he wouldn't stop, no, he'd stand at the back counter, high above the back bumper, in the center of the sign with the pictures of Cherry Pops and Push-Ups and Heath Bars and Dreamsicles he'd toss, one after another, out the back and into the arms of the children on their bikes and their skateboards and their skinny scabby legs. His robot would drive the truck for him. Major Domo. That would be the name he'd give it, the robot name. Every night, camped on the edge of town or in a secret cave or on the top of a mountain, he would tinker with The Major to add even more features. A squirt gun of a thumb. Jet pack. Laser Vision.

With the lightest of touch—a shoulder, a sleeve, a tap on the brow—Miss Conner uncoupled the line of children from the lip of the window that ran the length of the room. To the water-fountain, the pencil sharpener, the bathroom—the sign of the red STOP and, on the flip side, the green GO—she herded them.

Back to the window she turned. Drew the hankie from her apron pocket. Made a show of it, like the dusting of the window was a daily event, like the man in the truck, should he glance in her direction, would see it as a natural thing, a consequence of the breath, a woman of a mind to—at the break of the day and the brim of the glass—give it a shine.

The man clicked the handle of the sliding door on the passenger side and, as it shouldered open, stepped out onto the running board. He looked back at the emblem on the side panel, reached under the seat for a rag, then down he hopped. Set to work.

The emblem was a tooth the size of a couch, a cartoon molar with cartoony blue eyes and a smiley mouth and bean-sprouty little arms and legs like pins in a cushion, like a toothpick in a aperitif. The man wiped the dust off the emblem with his rag, then wiped the dust off his shoes, then, with the back of his hand, wiped the sweat from his brow. He was a young man. He moved with that extra bit of oomph the young give to all of them extra moves they make.

He donned the white blazer—the lab jacket off the rack in the back of the truck—with an extra flourish. Snapped the collar. Snapped the cuffs. He was a handsome fella, and he took pride in this thing he'd accomplished, this handsomeness. And the clipboard he carried, snug up under the arm? A list of the classes he planned to favor with a visit. He gave the box—the big box full of toothbrushes and flyers and fingerling tubes of toothpaste—an extra jounce on his way up the steps of the school.

Handsome is as handsome does, right? Miss Connor clapped her hands to hurry the children along. She was (in her own words) a *handsome* woman. Not pretty. Not (God no) sexy. Nicely framed. That would be the word. The handsome was not about her but about the order she gathered around her. That was the important thing. On her way out the house she'd always touch the frame of the door beneath the glint of the paint. Rub the grain of the wood, special order from the sawmill and why not, if that was her impulse, to own a scrap of something raw, the roughcut timber with the half-circle scored, the same shape, score upon score, up the doorpost and over the lintel in the house with the wooden floors and the Shaker chairs and the doormat fashioned, or so the vendor said, from a bolt of virgin wool. Handsome, see? Of the hands. The broken ripple where the blade meets the pine. She'd feel it there under her fingers when she'd cradle the frame, just so, when she'd loose the cat from out the house and over the stoop and into the blue of the day.

The blue of the day. The white of the truck. The sun that breaks over the pines to strike the—like in the ads for Duz with the extra oounch of whitening—vehicle. White like the flesh of a coconut, the flank of a glacier, the ingot of fire from out the heart of the moon.

"Farrel?" Miss Connor said it in the form of a question, but it was bigger than *where is your pencil* or *what's in your pocket* or even *what are you doing*? It was an open window, the question. Fling open the shutters to summon the wind. "Bring me that, please."

The *that* was a note. He'd snatched it from the Bergdahl girl and held it now, two-handed, behind his back. For the past minute Miss Connor (from out the corner of her eye) had followed the dance of the boy and the girl, the thrust and the parry. Prim little thing, Martha Nell, with the saddle shoes and the socks that pinched her in the plummy red of the flesh. She pecked at the note. Like a bobbin on a spindle, Farrel spun left, then right, then left again. Just out of reach he held it.

"Farrel!"

Farrel marched himself up the aisle and into the dock. *Farrel-land* the children called it, the patch of the flooring at the far corner of her desk where he stood to attention day after day, two, three times a day to once again—as Miss Connor called it—*explain himself.*

A haven. A land of milk and honey. He'd rest his chin on the wooden edge of the desk while he waited for her to rule, smell the varnish and the Pinesol and the coffee, rock his head from side to side, sticky up onto his cheeks the pencil shavings and the diblets of rubber eraser as he watched and as he waited. It was all of it familiar, homey even, the spot on the floor. His spot. Here. Where the bad children stand to await the day of judgement, where the soles of their feet sand the tile down to a tar the width of a cookie.

Over the course of the year Miss Connor had commandeered from him the hamster bone, the broken crayon, the penknife, the Rocket Racer, sparrow feather, bottle cap, gyroscope, platoon of plastic army men with the magnifying glass to weld them into a burl of prickly green.

"That's the price you pay," she'd told him, the sermon she'd offered up with every collar, "when you take from others." She would always pause here, for emphasis, after the manner of Winston Churchill. "When you trespass a territory not your own, there's a price you pay." She would elevate the sinful object, hold it there for him to see, to value, to weigh in the balance beside the what? Devilment is what. Chimpery. Animal spirits. The invisible whim and the twitch of the nerve and the hum of the blood.

On the shelf behind her, out of reach but in sight, there, beside the antique barometer and the biscuit tin all clanky with crayons? A season of loot. On the first day of school he'd smuggled a box of candy cigarettes into the library. Pall Mall (*Whenever The Finest Is Desired*), with the logo the crest of the king with the armor, and the red pepper of the lions, and the burst of the yellow star with the *Toy Surprise Inside!*

"This little item." She gave it a shiver, like you shake a tin of cocoa to tally the mass. "You want it back, right?"

"Yes, ma'am."

"Good. Then here's the deal, okay? You get it back the day the shenanigans end."

So much for noble intent. Day by day the collection grew. The wooden flag from off a mailbox. The collar from off a dog. The sock you fill with sand to sling—a sock-rocket—up into the blue. Private things. Snatch of underwear from off a neighbor's line. Birthday card with a blot for a name. The thing he found in the bottom drawer of her desk that day before school, him looking for nothing he could think of in particular apart from it belonging to her is all. *Finders Keepers*, right? She'd stepped out to shoo the squirrels away from the hummingbird feeder. Like it was the fault of the squirrel for being the squirrel and not the feeder for being the feeder, right out in the open like that, the red of the raspberry jam.

Tampax ran the letters in a mimeo blue up the seam of the white paper wrapper. A kind of a cigar is what he figured it was, that or a packet of que-tips. Whatever. It crackled when he pressed it, with the pad of his thumb, into the lunchbox, into the crevasse where the apple and the PBJ and the *Have Gun Will Travel* thermos nestled. Clicked the lid shut. He took it why? He couldn't say. Half of what he did he did from out a hankering to fill the empty hand. That's the whole point of a touch, right? To touch.

So no wonder then, when he showed up the next day, how smitten she was by his boldery.

"How becoming you look," she said as the children arrived in their Halloween gear, the class for the party, Farrel in the cardboard armor he'd elbowed into shape from out a box of Idaho potatoes.

"Space armor," he said. "A robot is what I am."

From an old bucket of Kentucky Fried Chicken he'd fashioned a helmet. Slits for the eyes. Gawp of a mouth like a Jack O' Lantern. The tin from a chicken pot pie torqued up at a angle and glued to the top. Radar! The Tampax he'd positioned between the eyes and stapled into place. She reddened when she saw it but said nothing.

Had she known where he'd gotten it, she would have what? Done what? Given him what in return? A gold star? A kiss? A crack on the noggin to go with the licks he got from that mother of his?

What she did was this, Miss Connor, what she figured was this: he'd fumbled up onto this little piece of feminine magic from out of a dresser at home, that's what he'd done, or back of the bath towels, or up top the linens. Or no. No. That would be too easy. She pictured him a shoplifter on the run, boss of the supermarket bulling up the aisle behind him and him doubling back for the danger of it, the fervor of the chase, the baton of the tampon a piston, a flash of the fist in pursuit of the impossible plunder, the wonderment from out the eye of the hurricane, from out the beak of the eagle, from offa the spike of the—what do you call it—Sputnik up there in the dark. That little blip of tin up there in the troposphere.

"Robot power!" he said with a roboty voice. Chirp of the bird.

She swapped him for it. The sleight of the hand. In place of the nose she (clever girl) proffered a brand-new rubber eraser, a slab of red with a slant of a kind you get with a robot. Deal!

Not that it made a fig of a difference a day later, or the day after that, or any many a turn of the earth to the current impasse. The battle of the hatchlings, the glitch in the whirligig, the collision between Martha the Queen of the Tattle and Farrel, the resident criminal. It was the custom—her custom—to savor the nature of the quarrel between the two. To let it simmer. The two suitors, keen, the each of them, to be the only child.

But today was the day of the Smile Contest. Another twenty minutes and the man would appear with the box of goodies, the buttons and the ribbons and the give-aways. It was all she could do to keep the children distracted. In a boil up over the bellwork they were: mugging at the invisible camera, goofing up a smile to set the boys to laughing, chittering on about a prize—a yo-yo, a Slinky, a puppy, a pony. Shameless. Unshushable. And here was a lesson for the ages, O friend of the tender. Break out the Crayolas and color the map of Georgia, thrill to the tick-tock of the time-table, marvel at the innards of a lizard: it ain't nothing but a bucket of air beside a stranger in a snappy blazer and a truck the color of snow.

Even she felt the pull of the clock, the spin of the sweep hand, the catapult across a now they never thought they'd ever see.

Farrel stood to attention as she unfolded the note he'd stolen from Martha. Ad from an issue of *Look* all mucilaged up onto a sheet of cardstock. Bumper end of a cowboy astride a golden palomino in the blue of a sky branded with a logo: *Levi's—Rugged as the men who wear 'em!* On the back? A crayon rendition of a… woman? No. Martha's handiwork. Of a dame. No other way to say it. A dame with a set of cherry smackers and a wristful of trinkets and a curve at the waist and the hips and the heels. And hand-lettered, in black India ink inside the ghost of a pencil guide, the title: *Miss Connor.*

Farrel's contribution to this fever dream of feminine zeal (*the improvements* he called them) clashed with the stipple of flowers that covered the goldenrod dress, the magenta blooms, the glitter in the ick of the glue at the buckle of the sash, the honest-to-God lipstick on the lips (Martha's mother's brand, *Satin Finish, the new Evening in Paris lipstick, there's a bit of Satan in Satin*). Ick is right. Not but a couple strokes with a Sharpie was all it took for him to obliterate the scene.

"Tell me about the picture, Farrel." Miss Connor beckoned with the tip of her pen. Thanks to Farrel's repair she stood on the deck of a surfboard now, in outer space, her head in a bubble of a helmet and a ray gun in her hand. "So where am I going?"

"Alpha Centauri."
"To do what?"
"Attack the Centaurians."
"Why? What did they ever do to me?"
"They stole your dog."
"Why would they steal my dog?"
"Cause your dog is special. You got a special dog."

She would save the smile for later. A smile would break the spell. Here was a treat all but hidden from the well-behaved. Brazen he was. Such a brazen child. She pictured the Blue Angels when they paint the sky, one two three strokes, the jets up over the stadium with their plumes booming out behind them.

Back at the back of the class, a stir. Martha Nell Bergdahl with her hand up. The fingers in a waggle. The outrage. The scandal. Miss Connor called her up to testify—the huff and the puff, the head to toe atremble, the knuckles all glisteny and red with the grief of it all, the upshot of which and clear for all to see: Farrel should be punished.

Miss Connor nodded, nodded and traced the outline of the curve of the hip of this Connor person, this intergalactic tart that scootered out over the page. She'd decided long ago the answer to the question of beauty was to refuse the question. "I'm a natural," she told the boys at college when they asked her why she wore no lipstick. "My lips are like cherries," she'd say. "Why would you paint a cherry?" Clever girl. Sassy. The boys at college said as much. She could hear them when they turned away. It pleased her to be—to think of herself as—a provocation, but when they never turned again to press her, to make another go of it, she began to wonder if her way of saying it (a harshness, as if the cherries were bitter) had somehow soured the harvest. Go figure. And by the end of a decade, well, what more was there to say? Was there ever any doubt? There's the fruit you pick and then again there's the fruit you watch and you wait as it ripens and falls.

While the children gnawed away at the board-work (*My Country Tis Of Thee* in cursive), she fetched from out the hiding place in the closet the treat she promised no, not the children, no, but herself. Promised herself. The print. From off a woodblock. A wave is what it was. A little rectangular ocean she'd happened upon at the Civitan Rummage. A buck and a half, the frame and all. She'd already prepped the wall (clever girl) with a drill, a molly, a screw. You gotta hang it high, right? Outta reach of the heathen. The nubby knuckles and the slickery mitts. The Huns and the Goths, the Visigoths and the Vandals.

Up the wall it slid. She shifted her grip. Cupped her hands to either side to push it higher. Up on her toes even, to where the taut wire at the back of the frame bumped up over the screw. Pling. Into place.

Behold.

In the small of the moment she wondered, not at the wave, but at the maker of the wave. Back in the day of the geisha. Up over the block of wood he hovers. On the neck of a chisel thin as a quill he—with the flat of his thumb—presses. Keen the blade. The every cut a perfect curve.

How did they do it, the Japs? She ran a finger up the slope. There. The spray of the sea a solid thing. The surf in a curl at the height of the tsunami, less like a slab of liquid and more like a, like a what? A buttress. A girder bent to the shape of a breaker. Fixed forever now the least little ripple, and up the slope on a roll the rowers, and itty-bitty the boatsmen, and off, and away, in the distance, the snow at the top of the tiny volcano.

A nudge. A nudge again to square it, to true it up. There you go. That'll do it. The fast of it all. To hold it—for the time being—fast.

Oh Miss Connor. *Beauty is a flower but only so an hour.* Even her shoes, so sassy the day she bought 'em—the stilettos, the strap at the ankle, the red leather button—betrayed her. Set her apart. Out and about of late, on the curb, at the crosswalk, in the press of the shoppers she caught it, from out the corner of her eye, the difference. Now the button a bloom, a fleur-de-lis. And the heels. A millimeter shorter. And rounder the toe. There'd been a change in the style she missed, something the new girls, they'd picked up on it, all of them, overnight, and now it was her who was out of step.

Not that it mattered to be a bit off. To grade on the curve. You grade on the curve. And thirty's a curve enough, in on the curve enough to call it—give or take a turn of the earth—young. She ran a hand over the hip and down the seam of the skirt to what? Settle the pleat? Buff the hand? Static up, from out the weave, another puff of chalk? She shifted from one hip to the other. Into the one foot and then the other the whole of herself she poured. A shoe's a thing you buy to bear the weight, true enough, but to the girls with a shape, a shape to speak of, it's all about the geometry. That's what it is. That's the thing. The shape of the leg.

And so the morning ripened. And so the minutes ran. And so soon—sooner than they figured—the moment arrived. Ten am and the clouds in a cannonade across the green.

What a stir. Had there ever before been such a thing? A Smile Contest? The children skooched together, squeezed off another millimeter of territory between themselves and the front of the line. It was an honor for Mr. Sammy—for that was the name Miss Connor read from the card he gave her—to travel all this way to meet the children and to share with them a smile. Mr. Sammy smiled and then bowed, a big bow, you know, like in the movies when the butler comes with the silver tray with the little envelop with the telegram that says *off to Bombay* or *we attack at dawn* or *Renfro was the one, it was Renfro all along*. The children laughed when he popped back up to attention. Even Miss Connor offered up a smile, sort of a smile, or more like a sketch of a smile, really, when you think about it, which Farrel did, and frequently, as he traveled with his eyes the landscape of her face. This was the smile she saved for occasions when the outcome was uncertain, the tug at the bow on the gift you may, or may not, depending on your mood, decide to open, the lips together in a line that might could maybe spring up (could you but catch it) into a smile.

The children giggled as Mr. Sammy made a big show of shouldering the reading table into place at the front of the room. A slab of oak is what it was, donation from a somebody uptown. The top a sheet of amber but the underbelly mottled with buttons and barnacles of gum.

Along the back wall the kids waited. While the other children cheated and elbowed and kibitzed their way to the front of the line, Farrel sifted backwards, to the rear. It was the custom to assemble from the shortest to the tallest, and a boon to Farrel, him being the second shortest in the class, shorter than the girls even, a distinction for sure, and worth fighting for, were it not for Jimmy, little Jimmy who was—with the red vest and the shiny shoes and that pompadour all spatula-ed up into an Elvisy swell—even shorter. How the girls doted on him. Plucked at his collar, clapped onto that warm little wrist of his, pulled him into line beside them. How they'd hug him, huddle him, cry out when Farrel would burst into the heart of the hoop-de-do to drop a Cheeto down the front of Jimmy's shirt, or thumb at his ear with the Elmer's, or body-check him into the boards. Farrel did not know the word and neither did he have a name of his own to call the hunger that hobbled him so. After all these months of trying to wrestle him into line, Miss Connor had a word for it, more than a word. *Ravenous* the word. *Feral.*

Mr. Sammy popped open the box and reached in to pull out a banner that read—blocky white letters in a bed of blue—SMILE. Below the smile, in letters all loop-de-loopy as a icing on a cake, *The American Dental Association.* Almost the size of the table, the banner sleeved out over the corners like a fitted sheet. When Miss Connor and Mr. Sammy each took a knee to tug it flush, they bumped heads. Bonk. Like in the cartoons. The kids laughed because it was funny—Miss Connor toppled back onto her can in the center of the floor, Mr. Sammy, ka-pow, onto his back. It was Mr. Sammy made the big impression. For days afterwards Farrel replayed the maneuver in his head. How Mr. Sammy flipped, in a single move, ka-boom, from a crabwalk to a push-up and then pop—to his feet.

Spry the word Miss Connor would've used if she'd had her wits about her. Which she didn't. She rubbed her forehead as if the konk had hurt, which it hadn't, not really, not with the puffet of hair to cushion the blow, ridiculous hair she'd surrendered, in a moment of weakness, to that pushy woman at the Encore with the Hollywood postcards and her *between you and me, sweetie* and *it's all in the bone structure* and the cigarette a stiletto in the pinch of the fingers. A bouffant they called it. A pastry's what it was. She rubbed her head to hide her—truth be told and who could blame her, what with all the kiddies atwitter—face.

Two-handed Mr. Sammy took her by the wrists and pulled her gently upward. How fresh, the starch of the collar, the white of the shirt, fresh like a mimeo the smell of the menthol. Sen-Sen maybe. Pep-O-Mint. Up she rose, up into the shadow of the wall of the chest of Sammy, Mr. Sammy. Up under the eyes looking down from on high.

"I'm so sorry." He lowered his face to a level with hers. Whispered. "Quite a team, eh? The two of us?" He smiled. The smell of tobacco but sweet. She pictured a man with a pipe, mahogany pipe, the bowl in the palm of the hand, the breath in a billow up over the knuckle, the shape of the breath a tangible thing. For the sake of the children she offered up a smile of her own. There we go. Upsy-daisy.

Together they sat, the flyers in hand, the table arrayed with the swag for the winners and the tin buttons for the losers (*A Smile For Life, Your Dentist Is Your Friend, Today Is Toothday*). One at a time they called the children up to give it a shot, to give it their best, *the old college try* is the way Mr. Sammy put it. Miss Connor smiled at the joke, the something like a joke they—beyond the reckoning of Farrel—shared between them. How sudden it came to pass. Already they'd become a *them*.

Mr. Sammy shuffled his chair another inch closer. Leaned over to whisper in Miss Connor's ear. She smiled but looked off, out the window and over the chop of the sand to the monkey bars that burned in the mid-day sun. She'd always been a clever girl. When the boys bet her a nickel she'd never reach the top, that the bars were too hot to handle (and they were: by three o'clock the tops of the rungs simmered like the tongs of a toaster) she'd smiled. So much smaller then. Little spindle bones. If she'd had wings the wind would've taken her for sure. In her purse (a birthday present, patent-leather red with a silver snap) she'd carried a pair of gloves. White. Cotton. She'd never even tried them on before, but they rode with the purse, right? That was the rule laid down by Mama the day they opened the present. *A matched set* is what they were—the gloves and the purse and the pearls. The pearls she poked down the mouth of an anthill to see what would happen. An ant volcano was what she'd been rooting for, but nothing much happened, and then it rained, and then she forgot. But the gloves. The gloves a kind of a delicate armor. The boys laughed when she pulled them on. *Little Miss Priss* they called her.

"I betcha a nickel I make it," she shouted as she climbed. "From eacha you a nickel. Seven nickels." Spry. How spry she was out there, under the sun, back in the day. She'd climbed in such a way as to keep only the hands and the feet in contact with the bars, and when she reached the top, and when they shouted back up at her *it wasn't fair*, that *bare-handed*'s what they meant, she hauled herself onto the uppermost rung, stood upright with her white hands waving at the sky and her saddle shoes balanced on the pair of bars that capped the tower, and shouted down at them *you should say what you mean*. People should say what they mean.

Side by side, Miss Connor and Mr. Sammy. They each had a scorecard of their own—a list really—of all the students in the class, along with columns for marking points in different categories. Farrel figured as much—he could see them ticking off, with check-marks or circles or whatever, the categories. They call your name. Scuff-scuff you go to the front of the room. Stand at the table. Miss Connor says *Smile*: one thousand and one, one thousand and two... The kid's got his back turned to the rest of the class, so all you see is the back of his head, and then Miss Connor says *okay. Thank you.* And off he goes, out the door to recess.

Farrel dropped to his knees and crawled beneath the tables that lined the wall. Here was a private tunnel from the rear of the class to the very border of Farrel-land. Here was the private view beneath the banner that hid the bottom half of Miss Connor and Mr. Sammy.

It was Farrel was the one to see Mr. Sammy move his hand. Beneath the table there. Behind the stack of give-aways and the clipboard with the scores. Lift it. Hover. Then bring it down again to rest on Miss Connor's knee.

There were these movies they'd watch on the rainy days, when into the cafetorium they'd herd the classes so as to give, for a change, the teachers a recess of their own. While the black air flickered and the projector chittered away and the sleeve and the collar stuck to the body, the teachers in twos and threes would gather at the door to gossip, or slip out to smoke beneath the overhang that hid the dumpsters, or shoulder up to the cinderblock wall at the rear of the cafetorium to lean backwards and to press, as if onto the flank of a glacier, the flat of the back.

There was this one movie, cartoon really, that showed the earth. Farrel played it over and over again as he crouched beneath the table. He puzzled over how the world, and every little part and parcel, was a puzzle of a kind you could—what would be the word? It was *take-apartable.* Even the earth itself, on the inside, like a melon when you slice it, the ball in the sphere in the bigger then the bigger sphere. Geometry is what it was. Mr. Sammy's hand on Miss Connor's knee, the hand in a cup of a curve to fit the shape of Miss Connor's thigh.

There in the dark Farrel practiced what his smile would be. It didn't, on the inside, feel like a smile, but he knew enough to know it was the teeth they wanted to see. Like a set of Legos: you click 'em just so, into place. He would wait to surprise them, that's what he would do.

"Farrel," Miss Connor would say. "Farrel. You need to smile."

"He's not smiling," Mr. Sammy would say.

"You gotta smile, Farrel."

And then he would do it. He would show them. Big fat nutcracker of a grin. Hold it there while they each of them'd scratch at the clipboard they'd agreed to share, Miss Connor with her Eversharp Adjustable Point Fountain pen with the safety ink shut-off and the one-strike vacuum filler, Mr. Sammy with the eggshell colored Tommy The Tooth pencil held (what with the right hand busy) in the left hand, at a chunky angle, like a first-grader, like it was a caber toss and him up there at the tick-mark fixing to throw.

They would both of them at the very same moment drop the pencil, drop the pen, rise up out of their chairs and—in the shock of the silence (the kids all breathless with astonishment) proclaim him, with a laugh and a shout and a shower of confetti, *King of the Smiles.* She would take him home with her. He would be her son. They would live in the van with the ice cream, travel the country pitching Dreamsicles and Chilly Willys and Eskimo Pies to the orphans that hide in the haystacks and sleep in the Teepees the Indians abandon. Up over the school they'd hopscotch in their hovercraft, Major Domo at the wheel, to shower the playground with jelly beans and peppermints and chunklets of bubblegum big as the dominos Granddaddy fingered the day he died.

Farrel waited for Miss Connor to look up from her writing. For them to call out for the next contestant. For the moment to pass. Did Mr. Sammy know that his hand was on Miss Connor's knee? Surely he knew, but think of all the places you place your hand when you don't think about the placing of your hand—edge of a table, handlebar of a bike, in the pocket, out the pocket, up the folds of the pillow. The hands, they got a life apart from the body they belong to, got a power apart from even (to hear it from Miss Connor) the mind they been assigned to. Like the day she got so sick of the boys with their sweaty mitts raking up every bauble in sight; the boys on a roll after recess, bouncing off the walls of the class like a bunch of baboons on the loose, and in she comes:

Enough! she said. *Enough already!*

The Carter boys dropped the coil of wire they'd tortured into a jump rope. It sprang back into shape and slinkey-ed off under a desk. Eddie dropped the bobby pin he'd plucked from Maggie's bonnet. The boys fishing in the bowl of goldfish stirred, stopped, and Farrel paused. Hovered the palm of his hand above the head of the chipper fella on the cabinet upside the teacher's desk, the bobble-head of Mickey Mantle with the xylophone of a grin. Like a benediction he held it there. The Mick in a quiver there. The class of a sudden quiet.

She swept into the center of the room with her hands up, the palms out, the fingers flung upwards for all to see.

The hand is not a magnet! she shouted, and that was that.

The power of the word! The unscratchable itch! For the next couple days, whenever she turned her back, it was like some kind of Magnetorium, Miss Connors' Room 23. *Magnet Hand,* the whispered incantation, the kids making like every random book or pencil or bag of chips, shoelace or hairbrush or muffin was made of iron. The wall. The floor. The skull of the kid in the seat behind you. Talk about a wow. To be in possession of a power that pulls the world, and every part of it, up into the hold of the palm of the hand. And here Miss Connor in the hold. And here the hand, and her not a move to stop it. Surely she could—if she was of a mind to—shake it loose.

Farrel crouched in the cavern, steadied himself to hold the pounding in his body at bay, readied up a smile, readied himself up a smile as he beheld, gallant boy, the stranger, the smile of the stranger, and—not but a stroke of a brush in the dark, not but a shadow in the stir of a shadow—the hand.

Ever so gently along the top of her thigh it moved.

Trimming the Universe

A Conversation with Alan Sincic

The following conversation was conducted by managing fiction editor James McNulty.

James McNulty: Hey, Alan! Congrats on winning our annual Adrift Short Story Contest! Dale Ray Philips picked your story from a handful of finalists. What did he have to say about "The Smile Contest" when he called you up?

Alan Sincic: What a great conversation. To begin with, such a neighborly gesture—an "old school" chat, in real time, with a bone fide air-breathing, heart-beating member of the tribe. He'd called a couple times the day before, but I saw the caller ID (Kentucky) and figured *bill collector, credit scammer, kidnapper.* Ping. Into the queue of the robo-calls it goes. So I finally answer and there's this moment, like in the sci-fi movies, first contact with the alien ship and me thinking, will this be the voice of an android, a recording of a voice, or the real thing? Which is another way of saying we spend so much of our time in a world mediated by technology, we've forgotten what it means to swim in the same water together. The modern dilemma, right? Born a fish but condemned to travel the sea in a submarine.

I mention all this because part of what we talked about was how unusual it is for a writer to hear first-hand the voice of the reader. You spend hours alone, or in a coffee shop, staring out the window, scratching at the page, up over the mug in a murmur like a conjuror who can't, for the life of him, remember the spell. And all for a heaping of words maybe nobody'll ever read. Most of the time the only reward you get is that feeling, when you pack up for the day, that the sentence or the paragraph or the passage you were working on finally, in the end, fit. You say to yourself, *I nailed it.* And then... nothing. The clouds decline to open. The voice of God in heaven? Otherwise occupied. Readers by the millions stir in their sleep, dream of sugarplum trees and dirigibles and ovens made of ice, gloriously untroubled by any word you've ever written.

And so it goes, right? The work will have to be—in fact, the work is, in the moment of making—its own reward. At any rate, for the time being. The consolation prize for the writer without a reader.

Which is why it was such a pleasure to hear from Dale Ray. He had nice things to say about the story as a whole, but more to the point, he cared about the language—the placement of particular words in the opening line, the turns of phrase, the peculiar flavor of the dialect. How rare to hear from a reader conversant with the craft: rarer still to hear from such a master craftsman. Pick any sentence at random from *My People's Waltz* and tell me it's not a piece of poetry in its own right.

So yes. It's the human connection that matters. We write to hear the sound of the voice we make, sure, but under all the static and the blab of the broadcast, isn't there, when all is said and done, a hunger to hear a voice in reply?

JM: Sounds like Dale appreciated the same aspects of this story that our editors did; on a craft level, this is a very ambitious story, so I'm looking forward to a fruitful interview. A number of words were thrown around in the editors' room to describe your writing: post-modern, stream of consciousness, impressionistic, quirky, purposefully dizzying, musical, hyper, etc. We'll talk more in-depth about a few of these words later, but do any of these words stick out to you as unfitting?

AS: *Musical* might be the best way to begin insofar as it hints at what (I hope) the readers feel moment by moment as they travel through the tale. A melody apart from, but in synch with, the particulars of the story itself. We call it voice for lack of a better word, but think of the territory you cover when you deploy the term: not merely the level of diction and the range of reference, but also the random impulse, the deliberate wit, the stumble, the trip of the tongue, the narrator at play in a world of words. Yes—I can hear the whispers in the MFA factories already—the language *calls attention to itself.* So be it. I say give the teller room to be as lively, as idiosyncratic, as driven by whim as the characters in the tale.

JM: Sure, sure. Fiction needn't be only *one thing.* There's room for all types, as this issue shows.

AS: First Person POV gives you this kind of flexibility, of course, but then you're tethered to a single character. The god-like Third Person Omniscient (that Very Model Of A Modern Major General) frees you to roam at will, but at the risk of losing the verve, the snap-crackle-pop of the First Person. Even in that blend of the two (Third Person Indirect) the narrator tends to flit from actor to actor, invisible as a prop-master in a production of Japanese Noh, ever careful not to upstage the give and take of the scene itself.

Plenty of beautiful stories in all of the above, but I find myself, as I browse the shelves, hungry for something different. It seems that, all too often, the narrator obliterates himself in the service of what people call the neutral observer. But the writer is the God of the page, right? Is it so hard to imagine a God as exuberant as any of the creatures he births into being?

Not that I'm any expert of the current scene. I don't pretend to know much of what other people are doing—too busy patching the holes in my own boat to take a survey of the shipyard—but I'm willing to bet other writers have gotten this advice from their elders in the past: behave yourself. Tone it down. Allow the story to unfold of its own accord.

True enough as far as it goes, but there's a difference between the narrator who withholds judgement, who trusts me to judge on my own what name to give the flavor of this particular experience in the offing, and the narrator who smothers, in the telling of the tale, half of what makes him human in the first place. A sense of humor. A sense of wonder. A bit of bewilderment at how we all (fish in the same ocean) manage to thrive in such an odd universe.

And think also of how the narrator—and the persona the narrator adopts—determines what we know about the characters. To tell the truth about a person, any person, you need more than the account of what they do, what they say, what they reason, and what they reason about what they feel. Half the time we have no "reason" for why we feel what we feel or do what we do. This is why I have such tremendous respect for the role that fantasy plays in the lives of the people around me. The fleeting thought, the flash of the irrational, the ridiculous juxtaposition is as worthy of attention, as valid a part of the datum that reveal character, as all the other crumbs we scatter to lead the reader along. The end result? A bit unruly. But by design. As I tell the neighbors who complain about the wonderful biodiversity in my front yard: *Whatever thistle or vine or runner the wind blows in, it's all part of the plan, right? Who am I to weed it all away to accommodate your notion of a lawn?*

JM: Regards the "exuberant narrator" you mention: I notice this type of voice more in postmodern fiction than anywhere. Pynchon, Wallace, even Vonnegut—especially Vonnegut—have these very lively, voicey, sometimes hyper narrators and characters who absolutely "call attention to themselves"—a style of voice typically opposed to the dictum of realist fiction, which you suggest the "MFA factory" embodies. It certainly isn't a dying breed, anyway; Foster Wallace in particular has legions of admirers and imitators. Do you consider yourself a postmodernist, or do you think of yourself as belonging to any particular tradition? If so, who are your masters and who are your contemporaries?

AS: It's a matter of taste, I suppose, and not a universal ranking system. From the tall tales and the folklore I read as a child (Dr. Seuss and Paul Bunyan and the *Rootabaga Stories* by Carl Sandburg) to Kafka, Beckett, Calvino, and Barthelme, I've always been partial to writers who have an eye for the absurd and a gift for hyperbole.

You could even argue that the fabulist is the true realist. Because we already have a label for the oddities that surround us, we forget how odd they really are. You have a hole in your head into which you insert objects that are not you. And then—presto change—they are no longer themselves. They've somehow *become* you. The writers who struggle to capture this sense of strangeness—the ball of fire that floats across the sky, the magical power I have to move my fingers by merely thinking it so, the invisible force that pins us to the floor—these are the writers who grab me, who remind me how weird it is to be dropped into a cosmos I had no say in the making, into a body I didn't choose, and stamped with an expiration date that, like a brand behind the ear, I'm never quite able to read.

Then add to that the writers who freshen up the language, the playwrights (from Shakespeare to Stoppard) who carry, into every entanglement, comic or tragic, a child-like pleasure in the play of words. *Playboy Of The Western World. Under Milkwood. Lion In Winter.* And the poets who write to be read aloud, the line defined, not by an image alone, but by the length of a breath—Hopkins and Houseman and Frost. And the prose writers with the flavorful voices. Whether it emerges gradually (*The Oranging Of America* by Max Apple) or boldly (Nabokov) or somewhere in between (Flannery O'Connor), there's a moment when you feel a shift in the center of gravity, the presence of another self with a stake in the outcome.

JM: You have a phenomenal sense of rhythm—even in your answers here, to a lesser degree; there's great lyricism in this story—and it never dies down. What goes in to drafting the language, the sentences? In terms of process, how do you work to nail down the rhythm of each line?

AS: Well, it's certainly a recursive process. Some would say obsessively so. I'm the guy in the corner of the coffee shop quietly uttering, over and over again, the same word or phrase or—eventually—sentence. If you think of the writing as a piece of music, a score, especially written for the wind instrument of the human voice, then there's no other way around it. You've got to audition every line. Is it playable?

At the same time, there's something else going on. You're not so much inventing a rhythm as you're trying to exploit the rhythms already implicit in everyday conversation. Robert Frost calls it the "sentence sound." As a writer maybe you riff a bit, like a jazz musician who capers around the melody without ever quite landing on it, but in the end you want to bring it back home again, right? Back to the thrum and the hum of the voices we hear, that—from the womb onward—we've always been hearing.

JM: Most writers don't "audition," or speak aloud, each line. Hopefully, seeing your work and hearing you give the advice will encourage more writers to do so. I often remind writers that writing fiction isn't a quick maneuver—of course there's that quote about it being a marathon, not a sprint; the time you, Alan, probably spend on a sentence is the time many writers spend on a full paragraph—or more. *Slowing down*, working through each line "over and over again" is some of the best advice I think a writer can get, simple though it is.

The time spent on your words is evident, not just in the sentence structures and rhythm, but also in your use of bricolage (which is far more often seen in poetry). You have a free associative style that shares so much in common with the stream of consciousness modernists—Faulkner and Woolf in particular, Stein too. What goes into making these tangential, tertiary connections? Do you ever worry, in your process of connecting seemingly disparate things, that you'll lose the reader?

AS: Now, I might be a bit addled, but I'm able to jump—in my mind—instantaneously from one thing to another without a frame or a tether or even a *click* to mark the change of a channel. That's just the way the brain works (at least some of the time). My guess is that a recording of this would not be particularly interesting to an outsider. But in a moment of excitement or passion or rage, or in even a quieter interval—a season of yearning—the random items orbit the emotion, array themselves, not so much in relation to one another, but to the center of gravity that gathers them all. There's a kind of quiet ferocity in Miss Connor—the hurricane and the eagle and the Sputnik, the Blue Angels with the *plumes booming out behind them*—that quickens in the presence of Farrel. Something about him makes her want something more for herself.

So there's an organizing principle if you want one: a surge of desire strong enough to waylay all sorts of odds and ends into a shape that—in a loose sort of way—resembles a single thing. Then you have to wham away at the words—as the editor whams away at you—until the *reader* can see it as a single thing.

JM: What do you think, generally speaking, about the want for a text to be *clear*? That is to say, what is your responsibility to the reader? The end of your paragraph there suggested that you agree an editor should knock a little more clarity out of you, or does lack of clarity often benefit the work?

AS: It's a tricky business. Unless you're dipping into the mind of a madman or satirizing the insanities of pop culture, you want to be coherent, engaging, and at the same time, precise. Patent applications are coherent and (excruciatingly) precise, but I'd hardly call them engaging. Too cluttered with particulars.

But it's the particulars—the sensory detail—that pull the reader into the world you've created. That's the conundrum. How to sort through an avalanche of detail to arrive at a clear, clean, uncluttered facsimile of life. Twain's got a funny essay ("Fenimore Cooper's Literary Offenses") that mocks a writer who makes a mess of this.

So you trim the universe. But now you've got to be true to the body as well. If our readers were disembodied beings, we could cheat on the details and they'd never know. But they're not. They're the experts. Veterans of The Flesh. So you've got to get it right, the purely physical stuff—how people move, gesture, carry themselves. Eat. Sleep. Kiss. And the "stage business"—who is doing what, and where they are: the entrance, the exit, the blocking, the choreography.

Of course, the clear is not the same as the vivid. The writers I most admire find a way to brand you with an image you carry to the end of the story and beyond. It's not merely a piece of information offered up to fill a scene. It's an experience in its own right. When Hamlet says, with a kind of shocking clarity, a king may go a progress through the guts of a beggar, the depth and the suddenness of the insight jar us. Knock us off balance. The idiom, the tempo, the imagery are indivisible, a single unit, impossible to paraphrase without losing the music that makes it all so memorable.

But here's the trade-off: the more meaning you pack into an ever-shrinking set of syllables, the more you ask of the reader. The pay-off ought to be worth the effort.

If that's the kind of thing you like. Me? I could live for a week on a single scrap (fresh-firecoal chestnut-falls) of Gerald Manley Hopkins.

JM: Trading off effort for meaning; our readers are getting a masterclass here—all great. There's a certain weight in your story; I've read it a handful of times now, and it always strikes me as—even when in Farrel's frolicsome mind—dense. It asks a lot of the reader, and I think you've met your end of the deal: the payoff is worth the work (and for many, especially us editors here at *Driftwood*, the "work" is enjoyable on its own terms).

Speaking of clarity, we spoke about POVs a little in the revision process (which all fiction writers—even contest winners—go through when they place a piece at *Driftwood*). The interiorities of your characters jump around due to the omniscient third, and the moment-to-moment switches in interior are very fluid—difficult to nail down. Occasionally we're not sure whose head we're in until we're already knee-deep in their thoughts. My poetry editor hates when I use the adjective this way, but I'd say there's some *poetry* in the transitions, in how fluidly the prose switches between them. One might say, "well, that's just omniscient POV," but you make the omniscience very intense and intimate by delving extremely deep into each character with free indirect speech. In contemporary writing, it seems POV/person trends have moved away from this intimate tact, no?

You and I had a bit of push and pull in revision about how clear the transitions from character interiority should be—or at least how clear the very first transition should be. Talk a little bit about the magic of sliding in and out of character interiors. In terms of the specific crafting of transitions and movements, what dangers—and joys—are there in doing so?

AS: I'm not sure, since my reading list is a bit idiosyncratic, but I'm guessing you see new manuscripts all the time—what sort of trends do you see?

When it comes to point of view (for what it's worth), here's the thread of a thought.

It seems to me that when you break the fourth wall and, in doing so, remind your audience that you're the god of the stage, you're inviting them to view the story—if only for a moment—from an elevated position. You're taking them into your confidence even as you remind them that it's all provisional—the set, the props, the players, the theater itself. You can play the moment for laughs (*Monty Python*) or insight (*Our Town*) or irony (*Rosencrantz and Guidenstern Are Dead*), but the rhetorical effect is the same in every case. You've nudged them into a new relationship with the work as a whole.

I think this is cousin to what happens with free indirect POV. As the reader you leap—or find yourself whisked away—from character to character. You're suddenly conscious—in a most intimate way—of the invisible hand, *the immanent will that stirs and urges everything.* Other things are happening as well, of course—the plot rolls on, the setting sharpens, etc.—but here's my point: there's something exhilarating about the leap itself, the catapult into the mind of God.

Pearl Abraham clued us in to this at WNE (her website sforsentence.com is like a master class in sentence structure). Note what happens when you read the first chapter of *To The Lighthouse* by Virginia Woolf.

Here I am, you say. In the moment rapt. I'm Mrs. Ramsay, I'm Mr. Tansley, but I'm also, at the same time, without losing an atom of the other two, this other self, outside the frame but connected by some kind of quantum entanglement—spooky action at a distance—to every little tremor in the tale itself.

Insofar as that's true, I don't know how to account for it. We'll have to call in the cognitive psychologists. What I do know is that something very strange and interesting occurs when you mess around with narrative point of view, something either disturbing or thrilling (take your pick) as you swim from one self into another and back again: just maybe the border between ourselves and others is more permeable than we think.

JM: Hm. I'm not sure I'd group free indirect in with metafiction, though I think I see what you're saying about how they both call attention to themselves (one with a far more heavy-hand, though); there are similarities. I tend to think that any writing with ambition calls at least a little attention to itself; that's what ambition does, and free indirect, in its intimacy, its intensity, always feels ambitious.

What trends do I see? Unsurprising ones, perhaps. Present tense taking over; second person becoming more popular; a heavy lean toward interiority at the expense of all else; plenty of summarized or "told" stories; sentences written in a form of shorthand; punchier, attention-grabbing writing. I could go on. Not all of these are necessarily bad trends, if well-handled. But I certainly don't see a ton of dense stories like yours; free indirect and stream of consciousness are certainly less prevalent in the works I read. Occasionally I'll get auto-writing, which folks mistake for stream of consciousness.

With so many turns of phrase and interesting language in "The Smile Contest," the seeming mundanity of the story's title sometimes surprises me, though it is accurate and precise—of a straight-forward quality.

Did you consider any other titles? How did you land on this one?

AS: This was one of the rare occasions I had the title before I wrote the story. Usually the title bubbles up in the course of the writing, a word or a phrase from out the flow that seems to fit. The difference here? What prompted the story was a real event with a name (as I remember it) full of the flavor of that particular moment.

When you're seven you take it for granted the world operates in a certain way. The universe decrees we cipher in pencil, scriven in cursive, queue up according to height. So why wouldn't you have a contest to pick the winningest of all the smiles? I figured, here's The American Dental Association. What do they want to see? So I faked my way into the finals with a toothy grin, then lost to an adorable first-grader with curly blonde hair. So much for the scientific method.

Of course, the tale took shape only after I invented the rebel child, and that tangle of the teacher with the stranger. Rarely is an anecdote alone enough to make a story.

JM: Is this usually how stories begin for you? An anecdote expanded? How does a story begin for you?

AS: You could say a writer gets hold of an anecdote and, by means of a secret recipe, fattens it up into a story. Surely this is true for some number of stories and, in a more limited sense, for any story worth a read.

Anecdote: the kids compete to win a prize for the best smile. Amusing in its own right. The set-up for a joke or a homily. Given the frame and a couple of cues, we picture the scene to suit our own fancy, in a flash, with hardly a thought. Which is as it should be. *Two sailors walk into a bar...* You're not looking for an orchestra when you whistle a tune.

Nor do you particularly want to enter that soap bubble of a world the joke conjures. The whole point of a joke or a sketch or a scrap of gossip is that we're on the outside looking on—smiling, whispering, detached, secure. But the whole point of a story is to smuggle you into the scene. What does it feel like to be a seven-year-old with the fidgets, in the here-and-now, in a particular place, in a pair of shoes already bowed and pressed and broken to fit a body impossible to govern?

That's where the story begins. In the dirt. You invest in the real estate the actors occupy—the furniture they trip over, the air they breathe, the way they maneuver that unmappable body of theirs through a world they didn't create. I might have a notion about what, in the end, the character is going to do—the man in the truck arrives—but it doesn't really come to life until I start asking what a filmmaker would ask. It's time to dress the set. Just what—exactly, precisely—do we pitch up into the eye of the camera? How does he exit the cab of the truck? Dressed how? Moves how? And then does... what?

In other words, you're not following a map when you write. You're blazing a trail. It's what you happen upon along the way that turns an anecdote into a story. The turn of the phrase, the local color, the inner life of the random individual—the impulse, the scrap of a memory, the hidden vanity. That's what shapes your understanding of the character, whose behavior advances the plot, the plot that propels you onward. *Terra incognita.*

JM: You mentioned Japanese Noh earlier. What other artforms and mediums inspire your work?

AS: I've acted for years in traditional theater, scripted shows of my own for Fringe Festivals and other venues, and spent a fair amount of time muddling over just how a given piece of work might play on the stage.

JM: Are there any particular plays, films, or film directors you love?

AS: I'm always on the lookout for that sweet spot where the earnest and the absurd overlap. In the midst of all the existential oddities I referred to earlier, we're all of us hungry for love, right? I'm drawn to the movies that honor—in whatever ridiculous form they take—our deepest desires. *Raising Arizona. The Big Lebowski. Brazil.* Even Chaplin and Buster Keaton in the silent era. *Heaven* by Diane Keaton—a kind of semi-documentary—sweeps you up in a flood of imagery, snippets of movies she intermingles with live interviews, random people who wonder out loud, *Is there a Heaven? A Hell? What happens when you die?* Brilliant.

I take it for granted that people in the modern era "decorate the set" of their daydreams with furniture salvaged from the big screen, the TV, and now the web. It's a human thing, not unique to the era of mass media (check out Hieronymus Bosch). You build a fort of your own out of whatever driftwood happens by.

JM: Where can readers find more of your work? What are you working on now?

AS: My website's a good place to start (alansincic.com). Links from there to stories online at *New Ohio Review, Big Fiction Magazine, Hunger Mountain Review, Cobalt,* and elsewhere. I'm shopping (to agents) a novel about flamboyant grifter and am halfway through a companion novel set in the same era.

JM: If I may ask, what drew you to *Driftwood*?

AS: Without a doubt your emphasis on careful craftsmanship, line by line—the word music. Your most valuable ally in this lonely business is an editor willing to give your work a careful read.

JM: I tend to think a careful read is the best award a writer can get—not just by an editor but by any reader; thanks for the kind words. It's been a pleasure speaking with you, Alan. There's plenty more I could ask, but thank you for taking the time to answer these and for placing such a great story in our magazine. Any parting words for our readers?

AS: I'm good. What a great set of questions—I feel like a racehorse run through his paces.

PURPLE

MEGAN SWENSON

I lie, spread out, across the sheet-covered table, and I watch as S. dips the soft tip of his penis into paint and dots it up my body. My toes first, all ten of them, which I crinkle because I know it excites him and he smiles. My ankles, my shins, the hills of my knees. He takes special care with my crotch, letting go of his cock and instead pressing paint into my pubic hair with his fingers, taming them into a neat inverted triangle. The color this time: a bright orange. ("There, that one next," S.'d whispered into my ear before at the funeral, sitting in the front pew of the church, pointing to a particular stain-glass trapezoid of flaming orange, the sun seeming to burst through it. His mother's casket lay open before us, and I guided his lifted arm back down to my lap, meshing his hand with mine. I held him there, and he calmed.) S. keeps the temperature in the basement warm because he doesn't like me to be cold, and he likes the look of my puffy nipples that way, but I shiver and they harden anyway when he gets to my most ticklish spots: the shadowed bony crescents behind my ears; the backmost edges of my armpits when he pulls my arms to stretch out above my head; the funky pins-and-needles tail of scar tissue on my right side.

Sometimes S. hums while he paints me. Sometimes a cartoon plays on the old TV tucked into the corner of the room. Sometimes he smokes a joint, lets it perch between his lips while he puffs, and the first few times I did not like this; I feared the fall of ash and burn. Now I trust him, after so many sessions. I stay as still as I can, for him, with my arms down at my sides unless he moves them himself. The cartoons help to distract. Once, I fell asleep, and I woke completely blue save my eyelids. "I wanted to let you sleep," he said. He was sitting on the basement floor on a folded-up blanket, waiting for me, an ashtray at his side with a still-smoking roach. (In the casket his mother wore a lacey satin nightgown, and a bright yellow feather boa encircled her neck, tight to the skin, to cover the noose's bruise. I imagined her rising from the box, climbing over the mahogany edge, unwrapping the boa, letting its arms swing like propellers in her hands while she strutted, barefoot and limping severely, down the church aisle. She waited for something, a reaction, a hoot or whistle, but there came no sound from anyone. She whistled then for herself. Besides that: the drag and pad of her feet on the eggplant-velvet carpet. Mostly, people stared at the enormity of her breasts, once surgically lifted but now, in death, sagging against her midbelly. But she smiled, was always smiling.)

"Hmmm, hmm, hmmm," S. hums. I look around at the collection of lamps pointed down at me. I blink in the bright and squeeze my eyes, gone spotty, shut. He stares at me, humming, sliding the tip of his penis, slathered in orange, from my right hip in a line to the base of my ribcage, and there: he has found my scar, the funky pins-and-needles, and I shiver. He touches the spot again the tiniest bit to keep the static zooming, and I open my eyes a crack to watch him, and he is there shivering with me, feeling the sensation himself through his cock to the crown of his head. We become a shuddering mess. Out of breath, S. says, "Want a break?" and I nod.

* * * * * *

It used to be different, before his mother. He drew or painted portraits of me, either standing or sitting or lying on the floor or the table. I was always naked. He took long moments to walk around me, look at me from every angle, kneel down to study a tendon in my neck. He was meticulous, arranging me how he wanted, and I learned to lie still. Each portrait was a study in color, monochrome, an homage to its own shade. It still is about the color, with me as his canvas, but it is warmer now where our bodies touch.

S. drapes over me a floor-length clear plastic poncho. I stuff my feet into cat-faced slippers. I leave them here at the house, now, for this purpose. They're an old comfort after the stillness on the table, and they make noise when their heads are tapped together. He steps up to the industrial sink, pulls the nozzle toward him, and runs warm water over his penis and fingers to rinse away the paint that hasn't yet dried. It takes a minute, and I laugh at him, watching him from behind, his head hanging so low to watch his progress, his ass flexed: my headless, naked lover. Once done, he wraps himself in a plushy robe and wraps me in another, a second soft comfort, the poncho susurrus beneath. Click, click, click, S. turns off the lamps.

"Meow, meow," my slippers say before climbing the basement stairs. The stick of S.'s bare feet on the wood follows behind. (I turned away from the casket, but S. remained alone standing over his mother, hands in his suit-pants pockets. I stood a few feet behind him, at an angle, giving him space but close enough to see when he blew down toward his mother's neck, ruffling the boa's feathers. He blew harder, then harder, his arms straightening and pushing his hands deeper into his pockets with the strain, his face turning red, and the feathers fluttered more violently with the subsequent blows. Spit flew from his lips, and the procession of viewers, I saw as I looked behind me, backed up long down the aisle. Some had taken notice, the sight clearly distressing. Others started to whisper, one to point. I stepped to S. and brought my mouth near his face. "S.," I said. "Let's sit down."

"I need to see the color," he said.

But he couldn't, I knew. I couldn't let him.

I squeezed my hands around his left forearm, urging him. "Let's sit down. Let's look at the windows." And soon he obeyed my tugging. The boa returned to relative stillness in the air-conditioned breeze. People came and stopped to stare for themselves—to up-and-down the dead woman, spaghetti-strapped as she was—and move past.)

I lead S. upstairs and through the kitchen, where he stays and I continue to the bathroom. He allows me this privacy. I hear him clattering through pots and pans in the cupboards, setting a pot clumsily on the stovetop, lighting the burner, setting it to high. When I join him again he shakes two unopened boxes of Kraft at me, and I tap my slippers together to express my content. He slices butter into a bowl a licks the residue from the knife.

"Yuck," I say.

He turns and lifts me onto the island counter and leans against me, giving me his full weight. I slump backward to hold him. "Hmmm, hmmm," he hums. I let him rest against me because I know he is so tired. I struggle, but I hold him up. I can take his weight. And I need him: he is an S.-shaped attachment that clicks into my side.

S. cries in many moments, likely and un-, like the first time he painted me, after his mother died. I was lying on the floor, arranged in a crescent, and he stood over me at his easel and painted great brushstrokes of me like the moon, dark gray. In the middle, he started to cry, and something seemed to illuminate for him as he fetched a pallet of cheap doodling watercolors—not very good for skin—and he held the pallet open below his face and cried into it, and quickly he held the pallet upside-down over me to see which colors would fall. A light peach, which instantly disappeared against my skin, and an aquamarine, whose puddle he pressed his fingertip into and swirled around my hip. (S. found his mother, hanging from an exposed beam in her add-on studio. She twisted slowly on the rope. S. collapsed almost instantly, and, the doctor said, went temporarily and completely blind at the sight of her. She was naked, had climbed to the very top of a ten-foot ladder to reach the beam, had kicked the thing over with great force and had broken her shin. Her foot dangled, and the rope twisted and untwisted itself, and she turned around and around and around.)

S. turns away from me at the sound of water sizzling on the burner grate. He gives the pot a short stir with a wooden spoon and dumps in the noodles. He tosses the powdered-cheese packets on the counter and pitches the empty boxes toward the recycling bin, missing, leaving them there. The bin is overflowing, other boxes and crumpled papers and balls of aluminum foil strewn around it on the floor. Things like this have fallen from his mind, it seems. I tried, once, to clean up after him, and he stopped me, said, "Leave it. Not everything matters." I picture him alone, considering the mess of his house, in the end doing nothing.

Once, soon after his mother, I let myself into S.'s house—with the key he'd had copied for me—and called out his name. I waited and heard nothing. In the bedroom I found him sitting on the edge of the bed, crying and masturbating, completely dressed. His penis he'd pulled through the unzipped opening in his pants, through the hole in the front of his boxers. He saw me and stopped it all, the crying and the tugging, and I touched his cheek, and we descended to the basement without speaking of it once. (S.'s mother had asked him to come to the studio, to bring fresh canvases, and with them rolled up and tucked under his arm he let himself in. The canvases flew from his arms when his legs shot out from beneath him, his eyes flashing blind white.) He painted *cunt* in sun-yellow over my abdomen, and he stood back to admire the lettering, and he told me how much he loved me as he traced over and over it with the tip of his penis.

(Outside the church, S. chewed three pieces of bubble gum at one time, his lips coated in sugared powder and dripping slightly with spit. People came to give their condolences. He offered no one his hand to shake or pat or stroke, so I instead offered mine, and I was shaken and patted and stroked.

The muscles in S.'s temples and jaw cranked against the gum. It squelched between his teeth. He pushed his tongue around his mouth, passing the gob to either side.

Soon, the condolences ceased, and people hovered on the church steps. Some talked to the priest, dressed beneath his balding head in robes, and on the street below a car pulled up with music pouring out its windows: classical, baroque, loud. A late-middle-aged white man was driving, and there he was halted at a stoplight turned red. He beat his arms and hands on his steering wheel, whipped his wrists through the air as if bowing a violin, banged his head, silvered hair flopping forward. The music rang its crescendo. He thrust his body against the sound. The light turned green, and the man drove away, and the music Dopplered down. S.'s gum plopped out of his mouth wetly onto the concrete steps.)

S. tests the noodles: scoops one out with the wooden spoon—a minute-long task—blows on it, scrapes it from the spoon with his teeth, burns his mouth as the water from its center bursts forth. He stomps his feet, childlike. I enjoy it, love surging in me, watching him stomp and whine.

He thumbs-ups over his shoulder at me. He brings the pot to the sink, dumps it into the colander he's placed there. I hop down from the island and throw a pot holder onto the counter because he's forgotten and will set the pot directly down, burning the laminate. His house is old and cheap. I turn the burner off after him, too, because it is another thing he will forget.

In go the cheese packets. In goes the bowled butter, the bowl to the sink. In goes too much milk from the jug I hand him and return to the fridge. In go the noodles. S. uses his fingers to get the stubborn ones stuck to the colander, and here comes a child-stomping over the steam on his skin. He sucks his fingers.

I tap my toes together and laugh.

The stirring of macaroni and cheese and the rest: the mesh and slide of properly wet sex. (We all sat in our pews, heads forward, except S.'s, turned toward the orange trapezoid, fully burst-through, now, with the sun's setting. We all watched: S.'s mother sat up in her box, quite nice, really, but without flowers, for she was allergic in life. Her right leg lifted up and flopped over the side of the box. Its toes reached for the carpeted top step, searched for its edge, but it was too far and so the leg just rested there. Its skin was exposed from thigh to hip, and the embalming had kept her pale, seemingly un-blued with pooled, useless blood. She pushed herself further into a sitting position, lifted her hips, and finally her toes found the carpet, and they danced for us, up and down, pinky to big toe and back, sliding down the white keys of a baby-baby grand.

Her left leg she lifted from the box with her hands, and on this the embalming was not successful: it was blue, grossly veined, was heavy and cumbersome. She heaved its weight, thumped it against the box's side next to the right leg, and it tumbled over the edge to knock against its partner, looking still so alive. She stood, strong on her right leg, very tall. She pulled the hem of her nightdress up, up, up from her knees, up to her thighs, above her pubic bone, past her hips, up to her bellybutton. She kept the boa encircling her neck, pulling it tight, but she let its arms fall down over her chest. She swung herself left and right, the arms following, and in the middle, come to rest, she pulled them aside to reveal the swelled and lace-decorated flesh of her breasts. She smiled, head down and eyes up, dancing for someone very particular down the church aisle. Not dancing for us. We just happened to be there. And S.'s eyes were fixated on the sun-burst trapezoid, the orange on fire, filling his church with smoke.)

S. and I move to the couch to eat with the wooden spoon, taking turns with it, right out of the pot. The regular spoons are all dirty. It is hot but cooled enough to rest on our laps, and we trade holding it. I warm my palms against its metal. S. makes a joke of trying to stick the whole spoon's end into his mouth, stretching his lips wide, straining against the wood. I laugh.

He tries to talk with the spoon in his mouth. His tongue flaps against the back of it when he speaks. It is too muffled to understand.

I am cross-legged. He sets the pot in the bowl of my lap, and I close my eyes and smile at its warmth. The sauce is runny, too much milk, but I eat much of it and quickly am filled. I push my palms down behind me into the cushion and lean backward. The robe slides from my shoulders, and I wrench it out from below me, toss it to the floor. S.'s eyes are trained on my breasts and their rustling with the plastic poncho, sticking to me. He takes a bite from the spoon.

"Almost forgot," he says, indicating toward the dots and stripes and smears and the words he's looped on my chest. The orange is bright through the plastic. S. switches on the overhead light in the room, flicking the switch near the couch, a small reach, and the fresh light bounces off the paint and illuminates me.

"When you were a kid," I say, looking down at myself, "you ever glue macaroni to a piece of cardboard paper?"

S. nods.

I take a fat scoopful with the spoon, open the poncho with my other hand, plop it against my breast-bone. S. watches as the noodles and sauce slide down toward my stomach, which I lean back farther to stretch, undo the folds in my skin, and he watches and watches and swallows.

But we are too full to fuck, and so we rest on the carpet. S.'s head rests on my chest, and his left leg curls up and over my thighs. His arm is flung across my waist. I have pulled a book from the coffee table, and I am reading in the too-bright light from the overhead, with my right arm angled below my head to elevate it just enough. S. is kind of snoring, but I know he is faking it: he likes to pretend to rest fully in moments like these, as if something about the world changes while it believes he is sleeping.

It is late. Nights like these, when he paints me, usually last very long. (She continued strutting, limping, down the aisle, dragging her broken leg behind her a bit, but so exuberant with the right leg, its toes dancing and tapping as individuals. When she passed our pew, she looked at S., stopped very close to him and waited, but he was so transfixed, still, and soon she moved past. The funeral's attendees turned in their wooden seats, creaking, the older men having to heave themselves up first, their legs haven fallen asleep, ballooned with fluid. The older women gazed in rapture. The rest: stone-faced, eyes wide, glued. The priest had vanished.

S. stood. Our fingers were interlaced, still, and I held on until it was clear he wanted out of my grip, and he walked toward the window with the flaming trapezoid. He stepped into its beam. He held his hands up toward it, palms forward, in worship, in fear, and he tried to come closer but like a repellent magnet was pushed backward, unable to touch the glass, which, surely, would have melted away his fingertips or stuck him to the window forever. Either would have sufficed, for S.)

I fall asleep for a few minutes. I wake with the book closed over my fingers, my arm outstretched, and S. up on his elbow, having spread the plastic poncho open and away from my chest and stomach—the tickle of this had stirred me—and crawling his fingers around on my skin, from spot to smear of paint.

"Shall we finish?" S. says, quiet.

He likes particularly the small mole near my bellybutton. He pushes his finger there.

I giggle. I tap my toes together, but they make no noise, for I discarded the slippers in sleep and they lie separated far from each other near the end of the couch.

(It all continued, and I wanted to weep.)

Click, click, click, S. turns on the lamps in the basement. I smooth out the wrinkles in the sheet and climb onto the table, and I lie face-down, bare-assed. To the table is attached a makeshift rest for my head, a cushion, a donut with my face in its center. "Hmmm, hmmm," S. hums.

This part, the face-down part, is more difficult for me. There is less to focus on, below my head on the floor, and S. does not like me to move my head around while he works. Face-up, I can work my eyes spotty with lamplight, or watch S. move, or stare at any number of places without moving my head. Face-down, there is less. And I cannot watch S.

He puts my hair up when I'm already lying down, as he always does, and he does it poorly, as always: the bun is never tight enough, but he tries his best. And I never expected a man, who has had short-short hair his whole life, to know. I offer to fix it. "No, it's fine like this," he says, for he really wants me so still.

This part, for me, so swollen with what comes next. I like to close my eyes, now, and I do. I like to hear him, to picture his movements in my mind. And I know him so well that I very nearly know exactly what he looks like when he glides around the basement, gathering things, setting them back up from where he'd moved them before, getting ready. Untying his robe and shrugging it from his shoulders, letting if fall in a heap on the floor. Stepping away from it, kicking it away with his heel. Bending his neck left then right to crack it. It will be a while of head-bent-over work, over woman. He cracks his knuckles, shakes out his hands at his sides, and with this his cock and balls move back and forth, and I smile because I can just see it all sway, shudder, return to semi-center.

And though there is less toward which to direct my wandering focus, when I am face-down, I can almost understand: S.'s obsession, the thing that burns inside him, the urge he cannot mourn away. He needs this. It is intimate. It is simple. "Hmmm, hmmm," he hums, at last touching the back of my ankle with his cock's tip. I jump at his touch, raw at the nerves. He takes a different route each time he paints me, and each time I wait, sweat beading from my forehead to the sheet below, for the moment that pushes him from art to kink and his arousal overwhelms and stalls the painting. The softness is necessary to the stretch and tug of his penis into its lines and shapes. And I, since giving in to my blindness from this position, feeling everything fresh, have been asking, with any twitches in my muscles or subtle lifting of my hips—I have been begging for him to give it up.

His mother visits me often. We drink tea. I tell her about the painting, because she asks about it specifically, and always she is so intrigued: she leans forward with her elbows on her knees, squinting at me, watching my mouth say its words, and sometimes she taps a ringed finger against the mug. I tell her of the color, the most important part, she says. I tell her of the long break between face-up and -down. I tell her of the desperate lovely fucking and the finishing of it all.

"He was always drawing pictures of girls, ever since he was little," she says. Her voice is scratchy. "And beautiful sketches of women when he got older. So many of them." She laughs, sips her tea. "I didn't want to stifle him. So clearly an artist. From the day I pushed him from my cunt he would get this look in his eye, very particular."

It fascinates her more now, she says, that he paints me without the canvas.

In my apartment we sit in identical wingback chairs, a pair I found at a thrift store, its basement packed so full of odd furniture that I swear these chairs were glowing, special objects for only me to rummage through and unearth, give new life. They sit angled slightly toward each other in my apartment, but when S.'s mother visits I turn them to directly face each other; when she leans close, it is very close.

S. makes prints of the photos he takes of me, after the painting. He lets me keep the doubles. I have strung them up along the walls, hanging from clothespins on twine. There are many. In all I am naked, still, and painted of course. In some I am outside, and it is night, and S.'s camera flash has brightened spots on my body that are horrific, and I am barefoot in the grass, crouched like some kind of animal. "Hiss at me," sometimes he says. He gets down low on the ground and points the camera upward, and my hair is often falling in my face.

In some I am lying still on the basement table, face-up or -down. These are the most gruesome, but they give to me the most feeling: I see the line along my left thigh that S. made by stretching his penis long and pressing it there, holding it, the touch that brought me alive.

On these visits S.'s mother asks for a sweater or cardigan or blanket to cover herself. She is always too cold and laughs about her nearsightedness in choosing the nightdress, the boa. She takes it off for me, and sometimes when she leaves and I move the chairs back to their usual places, I find a littered feather or two, and these I pin with the hanging photos, according to which session was the most recent to each visit.

With the boa removed, cast with a flourish over the back of the chair, S.'s mother brings one of her hands up toward her neck, exposed now. It is a reflex: She grips the mug of tea with both hands, then releases one and brings it to her throat; she gently squeezes, and winces—bruise still there, collapsed trachea still there—and she brings the hand back down. Next time, it is the other hand, and it cycles throughout the whole of her time with me.

Now, on this visit, she is antsy. "I miss him," she says. She nearly writhes in her chair.

"He would love if you came to see him," I say.

"It's not the same," she says. "You're as close as I get." And with this she leans in very close. I can smell the vanilla stink of her breath, and her eyes are clouded.

She leans back in her chair, and for a while she closes her eyes. "Hmmm, hmmm," she hums, so close to S. in pitch that I feel an erotic jump in my gut. With her head leaned back, she ceases her habit, and all at once I am witness to the horrid proof of her injury.

The bruise blooms blue-red and dark, nearly black at its center, lightening at its top and bottom edges, and it veers up toward her ears and disappears there. It is like a terrific storm at her throat, and I see swirls of clouds, fantastic and belching their urgent warning of rain and torrent. I am fixated, and the moment feels forever; of course, I have glimpsed the bruise's edge before, but I have always felt insensitive lingering my eyes there for more than a second, and now, seeing it full, I absorb its weight, feel its power. She is naked to me.

In a flash of alertness she is leaning forward again, and again I am breathing in the stink of her exhales, swimming in her cloudy eyes.

When the visit is finished, and S.'s mother leaves, her broken leg drags behind her, and with the door closed and my eyes open to the photos and feathers strung along the wall, all I see is purple.

FUNKY MUSCLES

A CONVERSATION WITH MEGAN SWENSON

The following conversation was conducted by managing fiction editor James McNulty.

James McNulty: Hey, Megan! Congrats on being a runner-up to our 2019 Adrift Short Story Contest! Your story received a unanimous rating from our editors, so we're all clearly excited to show it off.

Megan Swenson: Hi, James! Thanks so much for the kind words. I'm excited too!

JM: Let's start large and work our way small: the structure of the story. Talk to me about your decision to show the flashback within parentheticals.

MS: Writing this piece felt like flexing a bunch of funky muscles in my brain; the parentheticals just sort of happened. I liked the idea of having an on-the-page switching into that other space, like flicking a light on and off instantly changing the scene, but I wanted to keep the different spaces interwoven, so the reader has to let go of some expectations and be taken for the ride. I think the parentheticals also add to the weight of grief in the piece. The narrator is carrying around this horror that has kind of latched itself to the rest of her story.

JM: Your last two sentences in particular strike me as the reason this unconventional decision works so well; the formal break has a clear metaphoric purpose, rather than just a haphazard, idiosyncratic, or indulgent one.

One might think it a safer decision to at least break for a new paragraph before the parenthetical flashback begins, but there are times where your flashback begins and ends within a paragraph of frontstory, surrounded on both sides. I think during revision, there was one or two points where I pushed you a little to do this more often; there seems to be more poetry in the transitions when they aren't quite so clear and distinct. What goes into this decision—specifically: when and how to transition, when to use paragraph breaks and when not to?

MS: I think to a certain degree decisions like that come naturally, and there's a balance that makes them successful: I have to let my subconscious, per se, do its work, without analyzing it too much, but I still need to have purpose and know what I'm doing, thereby building trust in my reader. I agree that there's often more poetry in the blurrier distinctions, which is where the natural flow comes into play, the instances where the experience of the transition is more pleasurable than being able to logically unpack the placement of a particular break. In writing this I was also balancing the two threads in my mind at once—the present-tense painting and macaroni thread, and the past-tense parentheticals—and sometimes the parenthetical breaks felt right when the other thread was perhaps working itself into a lull, or a quieter moment, so the parenthetical, with its inherent strangeness, could serve as a relief from the A plot, so to speak. Both plots being sort of strange, though, seem to me more like plunging your hand into very cold water, then very hot water, and sort of going back and forth, so neither experience is necessarily less intense. Somewhere along the way the switching starts to feel more natural, and the sensation of each story has lost some shock, so by the time the two plots come together into the present at the end, the reader is ready.

JM: I love your comparison there to hot and cold water. I knew from the first paragraph that we'd publish this one—not because of the sexualized "hook," but because of the sentences and the shifting into (and out of) parenthetical flashback structure—all within the first paragraph. The paragraph has that *Driftwood* ambition that we love on both a structural and sentence level. There's a ton going on.

That said, the first few lines hit hard; I can only wonder what readers will think as they begin this story. What do you make of starting off with such an—arguably sensationalistic or shocking—hook?

MS: Yes, thank you for asking that. I've given this quite a bit of thought. For instance, going about sharing this with my family will be a trip. They've read my stuff before, and I've never been the tamest writer, so perhaps I shouldn't be concerned at all. Then again, this one has a penis right there up front, so there's that. It's definitely a hook, and there's intention behind that: you're going to read the next sentence after that. You just will. (At least, if I weren't me, I would.)

My writing will never not have stuff like that, though. I won't shy away from the body. I'm not trying to make readers uncomfortable, necessarily, but it's also not my job (or my desire, in the end) to protect anyone's sensibilities. I want to find that line that really excites me when I'm reading for myself; I want the body, I want sex, I want the crude to work with the beautiful, and I want to demonstrate that these things aren't mutually exclusive. I also think that work that is divisive, to an extent, is successful because it incites such emotion in readers. That's not to say that I don't want people to like the story, or that I'm setting out to ruffle some feathers; it's just that I do not expect everyone to like it. And that's okay. Some of my most memorable and effective workshop experiences were those in which half the class hated something, and the other half loved it.

JM: Some folks want writing that isn't quite so risky—be it in structure, sentences, or content. You've got all three, right in the first paragraph. Of course, convention isn't what we're after here at *Driftwood*, so the story fits in well—half of our editors certainly didn't hate it. We love the ambition. That said, I do want to push back a little on the premise of the beginning hook. Your point here is that it works: you'll continue reading because it's surprising or interesting. Do you ever worry than an opening hook is too showy, gimmicky, or in any way cheapens the writing? Why, in your opinion, does it fit well with "Purple"?

MS: I like writing stories that start you right in the meat of them. If I were to have started this piece somewhere else, then built up to the painting-with-the-penis thing, I don't know—that just doesn't seem as interesting to me. This couple has engaged in this intimate, unusual act that, as you read, you understand clearly as a way of processing grief between them, a way of expressing love and sadness. It's a sweet thing, though up front the reader is surprised, thinking it might be something else. Starting with that sentence and paragraph as a whole creates some expectations that I can later subvert, or otherwise challenge, which produces some of the truest reading pleasures, I think. And, since the painting is the main present-tense thread in this story, that first sentence isn't just the craziest part of the story that I throw up front hoping to grab you; rather, it is the story. The painting carries us through. That first paragraph brings you in right away to the story's particular mixture of the crude, grotesque, and mundane with the consciously artistic.

JM: Right. The opening hook is characteristic of the story; it's a part of the story, not up front solely to grab you, though of course that is a welcomed result. Hooks don't work when they only exist as hooks. They don't work when they exist only to grab the reader's attention—lacking in organic feel. In "Purple," as you've suggested, the hook is almost a hook by accident; the hook is in the premise of the story and you're just jumping in. You haven't engineered the opening expressly for the purposes of grabbing the reader, then doubled back to what you were really interested in.

MS: Right. Its success comes from working on multiple levels.

JM: Speaking of attention-grabbing, what do you make of the Freudian aspects of this story—the coupling of sexual acts and the mother's death and rebirth?

MS: The death of S.'s mother ignites in him a particular lust for his girlfriend's body, it's true, though I see it as more of a deepening of their connection; he's faced with the horror of finding his dead mother in perhaps the worst imaginable way, for him, which sends him into a certain grief that brings him that much closer to the woman he loves, pressing parts of his body against hers in order to create art, something that might outlast their physical bodies. Though there's no implication, necessarily, that he makes this art for anyone but himself. Perhaps that is enough. By engaging in this painting, he's bringing them together in something bigger than their separate selves, and it being made by their actual flesh, together, elevates it further. But, then, he's slathering his dick in paint and just swiping it on his girlfriend; the humor in it makes it accessible and humanizes him, I think.

JM: Could you expound more on that—on the relationship between grief and sex?

MS: I think it's not uncommon for grief to cause a spike in sex drive, though I won't claim anything as universal. I've certainly read many accounts of people whose partners have experienced great losses and have become insatiable as they grieved. It makes sense to me. Faced with death, it might be soothing to get into that most animalistic, alive headspace, where an intimate connection makes you feel perhaps cosmic, larger than the suffering of mortal creaturedom. Sex as a means to escape, but to escape into a partner, escaping into the present moment where the rest can fall away.

JM: Could you talk a little about writing sex scenes? What makes for a good sex scene, and what makes for a poorly handled one?

MS: Sex scenes have to be honest, I think. Overuse of euphemism is such a turnoff for me, lends a weird loftiness. (The word "member" in particular just makes me cringe. I imagine someone turning up her nose, looking down at me through half-moon glasses while she says that.) There's a rhythm to it, there's buildup—I won't typically write a sex scene start to finish, in a short story or longer work, beat by beat. Not all of it is interesting. Fantasy works well when there's enough room for the imagination, when not every little thing is spelled out. I suppose this applies to overall craft, as well. Leave room for the reader. But in the end the sex only works if it's necessary. Gratuitousness has its place in porn, obviously, but not particularly in a story.

JM: All good advice. Do you have any favorite sex scenes in literature? Who writes sex scenes well?

MS: That's a good question. I read a lot of Jodi Picoult books when I was younger, mostly because they're what my mom read, and now if you were to hand me one of her books at random I could flip right to her sex scenes. They stuck in my mind well. I think she does a good job with them, though I wouldn't say my sex scenes are modeled after hers or anything. I imagine I absorbed some sense of rhythm, though, through reading a lot of her. Also, Anais Nin wrote just amazing erotica. She does a fair amount of euphemizing, though I think it has a lot to do with the period in which she was writing, but the stories can withstand them, I think. When I moved away from New York, a friend of mine gifted to me his copy of *Delta of Venus*, and it will always have a special place on my bookshelf.

JM: Briefly, I'd like to ask about your reasoning behind S's name. Sometimes it feels a decision made in favor of rhythm.

MS: I think it does have to do a lot with rhythm, though it was definitely another one of those things that I just kind of did in the first draft and unquestioningly liked. I like the shape, its curve on the page. I wouldn't pick a name like W., for this piece, because of its bumpy rhythm. A vowel would have been less smooth, as well. S. just fit the character. It's got a swirly pattern, inherent.

JM: Could you speak a little more broadly—about how rhythm is crafted in your sentences? We're always telling *Driftwood* contributors that we prefer writing with an ear for rhythm, but it strikes me that rhythm is a difficult thing to teach. It comes down to sentence structuring, punctuation usage, and just having a good ear for movements.

MS: I agree with you on having a good ear. I love grammar, love knowing how a sentence should work, and I love building sentences with lots of commas, creating a sort of hilly rhythm, I guess, that takes you up and down. So much work is done in a piece with how the sentences flow. How a story physically looks on the page is a crucial thing for a writer to see, as well. Variety is key. Knowing where to let your sentences draw out, where to slow them down, where to cut them short—I keep harping on the instinctual parts of writing, and I think this kind of thing is particularly instinctual, but not necessarily unteachable. I think the best way to learn this skill is by reading. You pick up on things you aren't even aware of, that then translate to your own pages. If you're not reading (a lot) as a writer, your work suffers, I think.

JM: Agreed on all counts. It's funny you mention "how a story physically looks on the page"; after being an editor for long enough, you can tell with some stories which ones will fall flat just from looking at the shape of the first page. If the story is scantly written—quick paragraphs and reliant on dialogue to carry it—you know it'll skimp over the description and scene setting, for instance. Of course, if the editor is worth their salt, they'll read the story regardless, but the shape is a telling indicator.

Though it's largely instinctual, I do think there's a bit of a science to nailing the rhythm; reading craft books on sentence structures—Virginia Tufte's *Artful Sentences*, Cindy Vitto's *Grammar by Diagram*, Beum and Shapiro's *Prosedy Handbook*, etc.—and poetry craft books especially help. But you're absolutely correct—the best teacher is a close eye on masterful writers.

All of that said, you mentioned a love of commas earlier, too. And yet, you have a great variety of punctuation in your work; I see far too many writers who rely only on the comma—at the expense of all their other options. I noted, during revision, your use of the Graham Greene colon (readers: read the first page of *The Power & the Glory* for several quick examples). Could you chat a little about the role punctuation plays in shaping sentences—and rhythm?

MS: That's a great point, about poetry craft books. Also just listening to poetry readings, or reading your work aloud, are both helpful in that regard. And yes, I do love a good colon, semicolon, dash—different punctuation types offer different levels of emphasis, and they of course offer different shapes on the page, which goes back to that idea of the way a story physically looks. I think if you're someone who likes to build a lot of long, winding sentences, or likes lists, then employing colons or semicolons or dashes is particularly important in maintaining your readers' energy. It's easy to fall into a kind of lull when reading a story or book that's fairly monotone in syntax and punctuation. To be excited at the sentence level is another reading experience entirely.

I find it crazy fun to write or read something that breaks with traditional punctuation, though, as well. Or, at least, is doing something funky with punctuation. Hence, the parentheticals in this piece. By building complex and grammatically sound sentences—by demonstrating that you have absolute command over your language and the various tools it provides you—you build trust in your reader. Then, when you do something funky, your reader will be game for it. This isn't to say it's necessary to showboat your expertise, or write needlessly lofty sentences; rather, elevating your syntax enough to build that author-reader trust will then allow you to twist the rules a bit to fit your vision.

JM: I couldn't agree more, and I don't hear your thoughts about punctuation echoed enough in the writing community. Often, my favorite novels and submissions play with punctuation to a modest, precise degree—that is to say, not buck wild or idiosyncratically.

Let's shift gears a little bit to talk about the ideas behind the story. "Purple" is very interested in looking. Vision—the character loses sight at one point, in flashback, and it could be easily argued that the whole story is about the narrator watching S. Whether he's drawing on her, cooking macaroni, or openly grieving. To your mind, how does the story function on this level?

MS: I think you're right. The story is definitely interested in looking and watching, being seen in different ways. The narrator is engaged in some heavy emotional labor simply by existing as something for S. to see. She's uncomplaining, though we know she is struggling with the face-down part, has learned how to remain still while S. watches her. At the end, when S.'s mother's bruise is revealed in full to the narrator, she absorbs the weight of it. She is in a way blinded by that color; she takes on the burden of the woman's physical pain so S. doesn't have to. She knows S. can't see it—shouldn't see it—because the grief would be too much. He would never paint in any other color again, perhaps. He might never paint anything at all. Whether it is the narrator's burden to bear, either way, is perhaps where the moral tension exists, though I resist reaching for that. It's true, though, that the narrator loves and is loved by S. Their connection is genuine. She wants to protect S., and protect his painting, in effect solidifying the balance of their dynamic.

And, with the macaroni: her watching him cook for her, such a regular-ass meal, serves as a kind of relief for the rest of the piece, but you get to see her living with the little things S. does, like forgetting the potholder and pouring too much milk and leaving recycling strewn around in the corner. The familiarity of that interaction is comforting. Our worry for the narrator relaxes a bit in those scenes.

JM: One of our editors, Dan Leach, saw the story largely through the lens of repression, and noted how that factored into, say, the rich interior life yet lack of dialogue in the protagonist. What do you make of this?

MS: That's a good reading, too. Their relationship doesn't seem to be built on verbal communication. We also don't get the sense that S. and his mother communicated well, so then seeing the narrator and S.'s mother in conversation at the end demonstrates a strange balance. The narrator might be repressing the fullness of her personality in order to be this artistic support for S.

JM: Could you talk a little about the revision process? What did this story go through—from inception to final draft?

MS: This story has been bouncing around my brain for a few years, actually. Its very first draft I wrote during my senior year of college, for a class assignment in which I wrote something with a video of William Burroughs, wearing a suit and shooting spray paint cans with a shotgun, in mind. The first version has a man who painted with blood, whose wife eventually becomes part of the process when he starts painting on her. It's one of the stories I used for my MFA applications. Once there, though, I let it fall away to work on other things. Then, when I started my novel, I worked myself into a serious slump after the MFA—I started hating my book and couldn't get myself out of the cycle of guilt to start over. That was last fall. Then Christmas and New Year's came and went, and I just sat down and pulled that old story up from the back of my brain, and I wrote this one. I needed something to get my wheels turning again, a story that I actually had fun writing and reminded me why I loved the process.

Revising it with you and the rest of the *Driftwood* team has been a wonderful thing. I tend to rely heavily on my themes and points coming through without putting in honest work myself, post-writing. I pound out drafts and know that something, whatever it is I was getting at, is there somewhere for the reader to find. That thinking comes from the workshop experience, I think, where I would bring pieces to class and readers would pick up on those things that I was putting forth in the work subconsciously. So, revising it in this manner has illuminated for me what I was really trying to do with this piece. It's not like I didn't have command of the story from the start; rather, the process of putting into words the purpose of this or that element, in effect getting my analytic mind working again, has lifted my confidence. There were some changes that needed to be made—namely regarding the narrator and her early-draft lack of agency—and some thematic stuff to clarify a bit, and I think the story now is more successful than it started.

JM: My editor Dan Leach likes to ask what favorite sentences each writer has. What are some of yours, and if you don't mind, could you explain why?

MS: Here's one from Jeffrey Eugenides's *The Virgin Suicides*: "Years later, from the one-horse detoxification ranch where Trip Fontaine had gone to dry out on the last of his ex-wife's savings, he recalled the red-hot passions that had erupted at a time when he was growing his first chest hair." There's so much information in that sentence, so crafty. From "Sea Oak," that first line of dead-aunt dialogue: "'Sit the fuck down,' she says." That line just gets me. From Anne Carson's *Autobiography of Red*: "They were two superior eels / at the bottom of the tank and they recognized each other like italics."

JM: And what's your favorite sentence in "Purple"?

MS: This particular clause I like: "I feared the fall of ash and burn." I'm quite happy with the lulling cadence of that phrase. And this sentence: "She heaved its weight, thumped it against the box's side next to the right leg, and it tumbled over the edge to knock against its partner, looking still so alive." I really like the knocking. When I first wrote it, it had that just right quality to it.

JM: Speaking of that "knocking" line, I suspect some readers will see a resemblance in this story to George Saunders' "Sea Oak," though of course you tackle very different characters and topics and bring a confident writing style all your own. What influence, if any, does Saunders have on you—and specifically that story?

MS: "Sea Oak" is one of my favorite short stories. I read it for the first time during the 2016 election; I'd read a little bit, then watch a little bit, and the story was able to keep me relatively calm in a moment of severe stress. I laughed my ass off. But Saunders does that cool thing of writing weird stuff with a lovely, uplifting, kind of gooey center. It's impressive; he brings the experimental/avant garde to the masses with the relatability of his strangeness, I suppose.

JM: He did always seem an odd writer to catch on in the way that he did. But maybe not—I think of David Lynch as a similarly odd filmmaker who caught on too. Folks seem to like things that are digestibly weird.

You mentioned the 2016 election being a source of stress. How has politics affected your writing during the Trump presidency, if at all?

MS: Well, I was in graduate school during that election, and I remember David Lipsky telling us in class something to the effect of "things happen in the world so we can write about them." It was a joke, a mood-lightener, but there was such a weight that settled over all of us after the election. Fiction writers, in my experience, or at least the ones with which I most closely associated, are easily veered toward hopelessness, but we all kept writing despite that; I struggled to produce any significant volume of work while I was in the MFA, though, which may or may not have been exacerbated by the election. I don't know. I don't think it's useful to point at it all and claim it as any cause of my artistic struggles. I do think readers now might be more unwilling to pick up depressing books, and I do have that in mind while I write—maybe I should make this more hopeful, more not everything is falling apart—but my brain doesn't work that way all the time.

JM: Besides George Saunders, what other writers have had the greatest influence on you?

MS: Lauren Groff, Ali Smith, Carmen Maria Machado, Anne Carson, and Rivka Galchen are some of my favorites. Nathan Englander, as he was my advisor and workshop professor, his voice floating around in my head often. Michael Ondaatje's *Coming Through Slaughter* is important to me. I attended a residency fairly recently with Hernan Diaz, whose editor-style attention to detail made me feel in good company. All of these are writers that, if I were to have to whittle down my personal library, I would take with me without question.

JM: Outside of prose, do any other mediums influence you?

MS: Definitely. Music and television mainly, I'd say. Also film and poetry, to an extent. I watch a lot of cartoons—*Archer, BoJack Horseman, Rick and Morty, Spongebob Squarepants. Friends, Girls, Breaking Bad.* I consume a lot of media by just keeping stuff on in the background. It's a habit I developed while living alone in New York; it helped to drown out street noise and also make me feel less lonely. I'm trying to wean myself off of that a little, but alas, I'm often passively absorbing stuff that way.

JM: At the end of interviews, I always like to hit a few usual questions—a sort of lightning round. First up, where can readers find more of your work?

MS: In college, I had a flash piece put out by the University of Colorado Boulder's on-campus mag, *Walkabout Creative Arts Journal vol. XLI.* You can find their old editions on their website. Besides that, it's just "Purple." I'm very much an emerging writer, by most standards.

JM: Last issue, our emerging writer was Joe Totten with "The Starling Killers." I'm always proud of *Driftwood*'s reputation when it comes to this; we always have a good mix of veterans and emerging writers—always entirely by accident, too. I suppose it helps that we don't read cover letters until after we've voted. Congrats on your first full-length short story publication! What are you working on now?

MS: I'm about 400 pages deep into a first full draft of my novel-in-progress, currently titled *Before This We Are Nothing.* I started it in graduate school, wrote myself into a guilt-ridden corner, started hating it, then "Purple" came along and shook me loose. It's told from the perspectives of a son and his mother, whose lives overlap and double in ways of which they aren't necessarily aware. It has a lot to do with sexuality and addiction, but its heart is family and the lore we build to fit ourselves into a narrative in ways already written for us.

JM: It doesn't sound so different from "Purple"! If I may ask, what drew you to *Driftwood* in particular? "Purple" fits in well here; the story, especially in our latest, greatest issue, is in good company.

MS: I found *Driftwood* a few years ago, in 2016. I submitted a short story called "Rigor Mortis" about two kids who accidentally run over a cat and then take it out to the desert to bury it. Long story short, after a few revisions (and some major blundering on my part) the choice was made to pass on the piece, but I was encouraged to submit again in the future. I've had *Driftwood* in my sight—so to speak—ever since, and here we are.

JM: I do remember that piece—albeit vaguely. It had an interesting premise, too. Something about mysterious holes in the ground and a missing father, right? We have an editor, Felicia Krol, who I imagine pulled that one out; it's her type of story, definitely. But we operate very differently from how we did in 2016, though Felicia and Dan, as you know, are still with us; I'm curious how the editing process was with us back then versus now—outside of the more productive result? And I'm glad you kept submitting! This sort of thing—kind rejections followed by publications of a different work—happen frequently enough. Sometimes the opposite happens, too—a writer who has published with us before sends in five more stories afterwards and we turn them all down. It all happens; it's part of the process. I hope other writers who have been encouraged by us keep submitting as you did.

MS: Yep, the mysterious holes and the missing father. It's to this day probably my favorite short story I've written, but I made the mistake of submitting it here and to my first MFA workshop at the same time, so I was taking way too many suggestions at once and trying to incorporate them all, not listening to my instincts as the writer anymore, and I messed it up. It's a piece I will return to some day, maybe just rewrite from scratch; I don't want to lose what it had at the start, which was a sort of unexplained weirdness that made it fun. I threw drugs in the mix, on the advice of my professor (who is brilliant, I think, but wasn't the right reader for that story) which kind of deflated the mystery of it. I ended up bringing the story twice to that workshop, the second time with all of those suggestions worked in, and people were like, "Why did you change this?" Because you said I should. My professor eventually took a moment in a later class and said, "We failed you." I failed, too, though. But, I'm a stronger writer now, more confident. That first graduate workshop is hard. It's a mistake I won't make again.

All that to say—this revision experience has been wonderful. I appreciate *Driftwood*'s critiques being not so prescriptive; you said right from the beginning that all comments were only suggestions, that nothing would be forced on me. That leaves the power with the writer, at least in terms of keeping the story true to itself. The critiques, though, helped me see what the story really was in the first place. I'm quite grateful for this process.

JM: Ah, yeah. I remember the latter draft trying to explain away the surrealism—the heart of the story—with drugs. But—as you said—otherwise sharp folks are capable of giving bad advice. I'm sure I've given plenty by now. And yeah, writers need to have a decently firm grasp on the craft before they enter a workshop setting—otherwise they won't be able to distinguish good advice from bad.

When it comes to prescriptivism, we have a policy at *Driftwood* that we try our best to follow: always explain what isn't working, but never exaplain exactly how to fix it. That allows the creativity to remain entirely in the writer's hands, and it stops our editors from overstepping and coming in to write the story in the writer's stead.

Thanks for your kind words about the experience, Megan, and thanks for joining me for this lengthy interview. It's been a blast; I think we've covered plenty of topics and been fruitful in our results. Let's break out the Kraft macaroni to celebrate. Any parting words?

MS: None except a whole-hearted thank you, to all of the *Driftwood* squad. I'm incredibly grateful and proud and excited. It's been an absolute pleasure.

Honeycomb Beach

Nicole Zdeb

Your mother drove us all to the beach that day. Nobody sat up front with her, making her feel like a chauffeur, she said. Matt and his friend sat in the back seat. You and I curled like salamanders in the boot. We fizzed about boys the whole way. Not real boys, but the shiny young gods in pull-out posters in Tiger Beat and BOP!. Tom Cruise in his leather bomber and Kirk Cameron with his endless smirk. My father warned me that you were boy crazy, as if that were a communicable disease and you had infected me and now we passed the infection back and forth.

Armored by braces, a perm (It'll give your bob bounce! my mother assured as she burned my scalp at the kitchen table), and eyebrows drawn with Crayola marker, I never thought a real boy might notice me. Why would anybody notice me when you were around? You had a spiral perm and a full back brace for scoliosis, but I didn't care. Gold flecked your mossy eyes and you smelled like honey, even after gym. In Sicily, you told me, we ate honey straight from the comb. We'd get honeycombs from caves near the water and eat the honey while standing in the ocean. We could see Vesuvius from where we stood.

Imagine my surprise in the back of the wagon when you called me beautiful. The word cut through all my head static. I seized it and locked it away before you could take it back. But you didn't want to take it back. You are beautiful, you repeated and held my hand all the way to the beach. I closed my eyes to better capture the moment. Matt and his friend, what was his name? Jesse? chattered the whole way. Jesus, boys could talk. They were still in junior high, verging on eighth grade.

We pulled into Rocky Neck State Park and followed the twisty road through stands of skinny pines to the parking lots. Your mother handed Matt and you crisp twenty-dollar bills for lunch. I pictured my own soda and a large fry with extra mayo.

Your mother told us that we had four hours. She pointed to the mint green concrete showers and told us to meet her there. We grabbed a blanket, our towels, a frisbee, shovels and pails. The four of us walked over a sand dune, following a path through the sharp sea grass. Over a wooden footbridge, past the showers and public restrooms, over another dune, and there it was: the ocean. The wooden pier stretched far into the water. Old men with tattoos fished off the side, drinking cans of beer and listening to their radios. People packed the sand, pitching their rainbow umbrellas and coolers close to each other. Matt and Jesse wandered away toward the arcades. You called after them, but they didn't turn around.

"Where to?" you looked to me. I pointed to an opening between two umbrellas. We smoothed our blanket onto the sand, anchoring it with a flip flop at each corner. We rubbed lotion onto each other's backs. You didn't wear your brace during the day. I traced with my thumbs the scarlet crescent it made in your skin.

"Does it hurt?" I asked.

"Not anymore," you said, staring at the man snoring next to us. "It used to, back when I had a growth spurt in like eighth." The sun had moved since the man set his umbrella and his greased stomach gleaned in the light. "Should we wake him?" you asked, eyeing his reddening flesh.

"I don't think so," I said, flicking the sand with my toes. I didn't want to look at him. You poked him with your foot and told him you didn't want him to wake up burned. Nobody likes that.

We sunbathed, flipping over every fifteen minutes when the beep-beep of your Swatch alarm reminded us. I felt pinkish and ready for some shade. The old man adjusted his chair and umbrella. He was sitting up now, splotched stomach slouching between his thighs. I could feel him watching you.

"Let's go for a walk," I said, rubbing the sand off my feet. You agreed and asked the old man to guard our stuff.

"I can't guarantee I'll be here when you get back," he said, ogling your new breasts. "So you better bring your money with you." You grabbed your fanny pack and I carried a pail and our overshirts.

We walked back toward the dunes, found a rivulet, and followed it to a tidal pool that had formed around a drainage pipe. Seagrass blocked the view of the parking lot. We picked up snails and interesting shells to show each other. In one spot, where the water was a little deeper, a school of tiny black fish zig-zagged. I scooped some into my pail. I'd let them go later. We imagined that nobody else had ever found this tidal pool and we could claim it as our own.

"What do you want to call it?" you asked.

I imagined Mount Vesuvius in the distance, behind the bathhouse and arcade, shooting plumes of steam into the air.

"Let's call it the Honeycomb Pool."

"I like it. Honeycomb Pool. Hey, come look at this." Warmish water tickled the top of my feet as I made my way to where you were standing. You poked a shell the diameter of a can of soup with a hollow reed. No movement. You tossed the reed and picked up the shell.

"Oh my god, it's a turtle," you said, flipping it over so its underbelly faced the sun. Its skin was the color of chamomile tea.

"You better put it back. It might be carrying something." I couldn't tell if the turtle was dead. If it was dead, it was definitely carrying something.

You turned the turtle over again and admired its shell.

"Look at the colors," you said, offering it to me.

"Nice," I said, recoiling. I saw a turtle once in the road with bright yellow spots like eyes on its shell. This turtle didn't have any bright markings. It could hide in the shallows or tall grass, blending into the sand. Its shell had tan, fawn, russet, and olive plates ranged in stripes that resembled ribs. Around the perimeter, the shell turned the deep burgundy of a rubbed acorn.

"I want to take it home," you said.

"What do you mean? It's dead. It will stink. You can't keep a dead pet." I remembered the dead possum in our garage, how it stunk like it had been eaten from the inside out for days. Dad had cautioned me not to look, but I looked and saw the swarming maggots. Retching, I held the garbage bag and he shoveled the possum into it and swept up the maggots, some clinging to the broom bristles.

"Come on," I said. "Let's go find Matt. I'm getting hungry." The wind carried sound over the dunes, snatches of radio, children's voices, the ice cream truck's chimes. "Hear that? Come on."

"I want to take it home," you repeated.

"But it's dead," I answered. "Your mom will never let you keep a dead turtle." I reached into the water and picked up a smooth indigo stone. A ribbon of lighter quartz ran through it.

"Look at this," I handed it to you, but you ignored my offering. I put the stone in my pail. I would give it to you later.

"You're right. I can't have a dead turtle. I'll just keep the shell. Hold it." You held the turtle out to me. "I'll get a stick."

You dropped the turtle into the pail on top of the tiny black fish and my stone. It struck me that we didn't know if the turtle was dead. Maybe it was just playing dead. I sniffed the pail. It smelled like jellybeans and coconut suntan oil.

You came back empty handed.

"No sticks," you said.

"Well, that's okay," I said, tipping the pail to dump the turtle and fish and stone.

"Hold on," you directed. "We can use our shovels. Flip it over."

I froze. You grabbed the pail from my hands and tipped it over. The tiny black fish spilled onto the sand and you caught the turtle in your palm. Tossing the pail, you handed me the turtle.

"Like this," you said.

I held the turtle's shell and you stabbed it with the pink plastic shovel. My hands bobbed down with each stab. Its legs convulsed each time the shovel hit its body, but the skin didn't break.

"I need a solid surface," you said, looking around. "Here, hold it on the drainage pipe."

You grabbed the turtle and put it upside down on the pipe. Not making eye contact, you focused on the turtle with eyebrows drawn and lips turned downward. I could see that you would look like your mother one day.

"Hold it still," you said, and I held it still. Each blow vibrated the drainpipe. You stabbed and stabbed and finally its skin broke. I could hear the small sound of skin tearing open. A black ribbon of guts poked through. You grabbed it with your fingers, pulled out a veined gut clot, tossed it into the water, and reached your fingers into the slit for more. I watch the guts in the water float and uncurl in slow motion. You grabbed the shell out of my hands, saying you needed better traction.

"Look at that." I looked and saw one turtle arm hanging by a strip of skin. It's the only arm I could see. I wondered if you had ripped off the other limbs, torn and tossed them into the salty water.

"Do you have my asthma medicine?" you wheezed. "I can't breathe."

I said that it's in your fanny pack. You remembered you were wearing the fanny pack, took out your inhaler, and puffed. Usually when you have an asthma attack, I cup my palms and gently strike your back. You say it feels good. I put my head against your back once and heard the wheezing in your lung, like a hummingbird inside you.

"It's almost done," you said once you could breathe again. "Just need to scrape it a little more." You looked around and saw a mussel shell. I looked at the remains of the turtle in your hand. Only the shell survived.

"Perfect tool," you said. You held the indigo blue shell firmly in one hand and the turtle shell in the other and scraped the shell until smooth.

You held the turtle shell out. There's a dark line around the shell where the skin connected. Most of the skin was scraped except a few shreds on each side. The glossy innards were gone. The shell looked smaller without the rest of the body, not much bigger than a sand dollar.

"Shit, I broke it," you said, pointing to the visible crack down the shell where the spine would be. You tossed the emptied shell onto the ground. Maybe a hermit crab would find it, maybe it would become its home. I reached for the shell and put it in my pail. I carried that broken shell with me for a decade, from apartment to apartment, city to city. It's an ashtray by the time I'm ready to move to the Vineyard.

"Let's go," you said, leading the way through the dunes to the boardwalk. "I'm starving. Aren't you?" I followed your stiff back along the boardwalk, up the hill, and into the arcade. Engrossed in Space Invaders, Matt and Jesse didn't notice us right away. When they finally did, I remembered our overshirts and put mine on. You shivered and put yours on, too. I noticed the sunburn on your shoulders. We ordered hot dogs and fries. The beads of condensation rolled over my fingers as I grabbed the bottle of Coke.

"Wanna play frisbee?" Matt asked as we finished lunch.

"Sure," I said, sucking on my Coke. I didn't care what we did. I was ready to go home. Back at our blanket, you took off your overshirt. A heat rash bloomed across your back and torso, tiny red dots and pink welts.

"What is that?" you ask. "Is it sunburn?"

"I don't know. Maybe it is." It looked a lot worse than sunburn and you should have put your shirt back on, but I didn't feel like talking.

We waded into the ocean until it reached our belly buttons. The ocean bottom felt soft as skin and I didn't want my feet to touch it. I moved out where the water was over my head and treaded. Seaweed streamers covered my arms.

"Wow, you can really tread water," Matt called to me. I didn't answer and moved farther out. I knew I wouldn't drown if I kept moving my legs in slow, rhythmic circles until it was time to go home. He threw the Frisbee at me, but it fell short. He waited for me to move toward it, but I didn't move. I treaded in place and imagined the sea monsters beneath my legs. He lunged toward the floating red disc, eyes wide at being in the ocean over his head.

Fidelity to Childhood

A Conversation with Nicole Zdeb

The following conversation was conducted by managing fiction editor James McNulty.

James McNulty: Hey, Nicole! Thanks for joining the pages of *Driftwood*! I'm excited to finally get this story out into the world!

Nicole Zdeb: Thank you for your patience and your close reading.

JM: Let's kick off easy. We've read a lot of stories about children here at *Driftwood*—and we've published a good number of them. To your mind, what makes a story about children successful? What makes it difficult to write?

NZ: There's a distinction between a story that has children in it and a story about children. There's a further distinction between a story about *children* and a story about *childhood*.

It's impossible to remember with fidelity (not that we can remember anything with fidelity, but that's a different discussion) what childhood was like because our capacities have changed through the developmental process. Our linguistic and cognitive capacities have developed; our cultural and philosophical frameworks are constructed; our relationship with mortality is established. We engage in the social, historical, and cultural dialogue in a way that is simply impossible during childhood. We have different brains as adults.

In my memory, childhood was a theater of cruelty, filled with outlandish fears, powerlessness, and wonder. I think successful stories about childhood capture this cruelty. There's the bowdlerized version of childhood where little humans splash in puddles and wish on stars and enchant with their ability to invest the world with magic, and then there's the reality that childhood was messy. Children are monsters sometimes. They pull wings off living things; they burn insects alive; they drown and kill with a sense of impunity until they are taught to suppress these impulses. They wield their innate power as apex creatures until socialized. Most adults who have been successfully socialized control this cruelty, or bury it, or transform it.

Simply put, it's difficult to write about childhood because you can't relive it. It's a lost continent. You can't unread Shakespeare or unlearn the tremendous amount of cultural transmission that you have absorbed in the intervening years. What was it like to move through the world before you knew all that? Impossible to retrieve, so you imagine what it was like. Maybe you capture something that feels slightly authentic and maybe you don't.

It's difficult to write about children because they are not "little adults." They are a different thing. A caterpillar is not a little butterfly. It's a different thing.

There's the urge to either infantilize children or make them overly precocious, to idealize and flatten them, to uncomplicate them, or to make them the vehicles for larger truths, to render them symbols. All of these are traps.

JM: How'd you come up with this premise—two girls exploring the beach, eventually finding and desecrating a dead turtle?

NZ: I have no idea. Where do ideas come from? The flotsam and jetsam of a life. I can trace certain veins in the story. The beach itself is a real place. It's Rocky Neck State Park in Connecticut, one of my favorite places as a young person. I had incredible experiences there interacting with nature and testing my boundaries. I'd play with dead things and living things and learn about both. It was a classroom, a lab, and an escape from the limits of my being. In the ocean, I felt free. Also, terrified. I almost drowned once in the water and have never forgotten what that felt like. I became a lifeguard in my teen years because of it. I also believed that I could breathe underwater until I nearly drowned. I had memories of breathing underwater, of flying through the water. Where did they come from? To this day, I love mermaids. Who doesn't, right?

JM: Could we talk a little about what second person adds to this story? The protagonist has some confused feelings about the "you" character—especially by the story's end. How does second person play into that?

NZ: The protagonist learns through the course of the story that the "you" character is capable of a wide range of expressions, from tenderness to cruelty. The protagonist learns that relationships are a complicated negotiation between the Other and the Self. Someone that you love and identify with can act in a way that you don't love and don't want to identify with, so it's about understanding the distances and boundaries that exist between humans. "You" are you, and "I" am me, and the twain shall never meet. That is a big lesson, or at least it was for me.

JM: In fiction studies, there's plenty of debate about nameless protagonists; some argue that a nameless protagonist is more universal and identifiable, whereas others argue that specificity is key to empathy. Why'd you decide to go with a nameless protagonist?

NZ: It flows from the first-person narration. How often do you think of yourself as a named person? I am not *Nicole* in my mind. That's an identifier for others to use. Who the hell's *Nicole*? Beats me. I've never met her. To know the character's name is to know something trivial that feels important but isn't. Names are deceiving like that. Empty containers.

JM: You do a great job of showing us a window into the character by noting *what she observes*. We're drenched in her perspective in ways that aren't immediately noticeable. The final line is a good example. Obviously, it's the protagonist, not Matt, who is "over [her] head," but she projects this onto Matt. Talk a little bit about how you reveal character and how first person narration plays into that.

NZ: This character isn't revealed by what she says or what other characters say about her. She's somewhat revealed by what she does. She's mostly revealed by what she sees. It's an intimacy that is supported by first person narration. You walk in her shoes, so to speak. There's something cinematic about it. There are moments when the intimacy is broken, when the narrative voice comes from farther away and moves through time, reflects, contextualizes, but mostly, there's the immediacy and intimacy of being someone's eyes. You see the world as she does and draw your own conclusions.

JM: Could you talk to me about the drafting process? How much work went into the creation of the story as we see it here?

NZ: This story came from an assignment for class with Natalie Serber, a Portland-based author and teacher, to write a story about a journey. I don't remember the drafting process. Frankly, I don't remember writing it, but that's not unusual. I often don't remember what I've written. I'll read it the next day or week or year and wonder where it came from. Sometimes I don't even recognize what I've written. It's a mystery to me, and I'm okay with dwelling in that place of mystery.

JM: What other writers inspired "Honeycomb Beach"?

NZ: Nobody that I can think to name. I don't know where my work comes from—it flows from a place that feels instinctual, sometimes vatic. It's almost a channeling process. I sit down, empty my mind, and let words flow out of my fingers. In time, I am sure I will get more intentional or controlled. Or maybe not. I've been writing for thirty-five years and it hasn't happened yet. That said, studying fiction the past year and a half and interacting with fiction writers has been eye opening. The process feels very different. I studied poetry at Iowa and feel like I can talk about poetry in a way that I just can't yet about fiction.

JM: You mentioned earlier the term "cinematic"; what other mediums have influenced your work?

NZ: I am a poet, through and through. I've been writing poetry since I was ten years old. I've been writing fiction for less than two years. Fiction is like climbing a sheer cliff without ropes for me. It's the hardest and most exhausting thing I've done creatively. "Honeycomb Beach" is maybe the second short story I've ever written. I don't know what inspired me to start down that path. One day I woke up and said, *I want to write stories.* I'm a novice, an apprentice, a child in Fictionland. It's humbling.

In terms of mediums other than poetry, I dabble in painting and photography. Visual arts, particularly painting, have influenced my work, but nothing has influenced me as much as poetry. It was the key to my inner world and the filter through which I have tried to organize and make sense of my life.

JM: It makes sense that you're a poet; there's a clear attention to words, phrasing, and rhythm in this story that isn't incredibly common in fiction writers (though is, of course, common in *Driftwood* writers). What are you working on now? Any fiction?

NZ: I'm eighty thousand words into a novel that will likely never see the light of day. I'm also working on a poetry chapbook called *Luminous Blue Variable.* It's an origin myth of sorts. I'm adopted and my genesis has always been murky. This work is a way of addressing that and maybe healing. I'm planting words in that big hole that exists when I look into my past. We'll see what blooms. I'm also shopping around my poetry manuscript, *The Occupied Woman.*

JM: I hope your novel *does* see the light of day. It's a remarkable feat to have your second short story ever written published, so I'm certain the novel will be worth pursuing. Your background in poetry has given you a great head start. Any parting words to leave with our readers?

NZ: I'd like to thank them for supporting *Driftwood* and other journals and literary presses. It enriches the cultural dialogue to have small and independent outlets that can take risks and don't have to pander to advertisers and the dominant paradigm. I'd also like to thank Beth Kern, my eighth grade teacher. She encouraged us to write in class every day and have fun with it. She made a difference in this girl's life. Thank you, Beth, wherever you are. And thank you to all the teachers who might be reading this. You make the world a better place.

THE SETTING OF SMALL FIRES

MATTHEW RICKART

Even in the late summer, the temperature was never that hot. But that's what the neighbors said when they left in droves for months at the shore. "With the weather and all…" and "Jesus, but this heat..." they'd tell my mom at the grocery store or car wash, then be gone within the week.

Syrie and I watched our neighborhood vacate itself. Station wagons wobbling, puttering under the weight of families. We watched from the hedges of her yard, the picket fence of mine. When the last car left, we packed a dinner in one large paper sack and explored. We learned tentatively, day-to-day, who was still home, who was not. Most houses were empty. Syrie threw stones at windows, waited for blinds to part; she peeked into garages while standing on milk crates. In the evenings, we ate chicken sandwiches and potato chips, shared a thermos of lemonade. The chips cut our mouths and the lemonade sweetly stung.

We sat on the hills behind nos. 431, 433 and 435 Cañada Drive and played gin rummy 'til dark. When lights didn't turn on in all three, we made a choice. Slapjack helped decide between 431 and 435. Syrie won. We ran down the hill to 435, the moon high overhead like a ripe orange.

That night we just jiggled door handles. Syrie wrote "435 Cañada" in her notebook, as if we wouldn't be thinking of it every waking moment before sleep.

The next morning, mom packed peanut butter and banana sandwiches, put a bright purple plum in each. Syrie hated peanut butter, but it didn't matter that day.

"You keep all your eyes open," said mom, as though I had more than two. "Radio man warned about suspicious activity, gangs of thieves looking for empty houses."

I was eleven, and it all sounded super exciting. I wished I'd more than two eyes.

I found Syrie leaning on her mailbox, and we walked the half-mile to the hill. Syrie brought a book with her, tiny and worn with grease stains on the cover. *Working Woman's Guide to Basic Household Mechanics*. She'd dog-eared a page about picking locks. I read aloud as she jimmied no. 435's bulkhead. It took twenty minutes, many diagram references. But when she sprang the lock, we cheered, nearly hugged.

A small basement, like most houses on Cañada. Stacks of boxes, rows of dresses on hangers, cords of firewood. In the kitchen, Syrie drank two tumblers of tap water. We commented on fridge magnets, photos. One of Christ, heart illuminated in flame and tied up in thorns. "Looks like barbwire and barbecue," Syrie said.

"Looks like someone set his heart on fire," I said.

The scent of mothballs. Syrie opened bedroom windows. We lied on the top covers, sea-like blue. Floating. Syrie fell asleep and I set my wristwatch alarm. I didn't dream so much as witnessed a series of images: a circus man, the desert, a garbage pail aflame. When I woke, Syrie was staring at the ceiling. "Have you ever been to the beach?" she asked.

We were kids. What games did we play? When other kids played with us, I only wanted to be on Syrie's team, her attention like warm light in November. But just us now, our games became weirder, more personal, esoteric and filled with private vocabulary.

We were daylight haunters, Syrie said. We told each other we were ghosts, we had just met, our lives were past and replaced by total recall. Syrie said she had been Otis Redding. Georgian childhood, brief success, a contract requiring her voice to plead when it sings. She told me about the plane crash with a vividness that'd make an adult blanche.

In no. 435, Syrie put on a record and made up her own words to the instrumentals, syrupy with words like "mercy" and "darlin love." Quarts of ice cream in the freezer, large wooden stirring spoons. After, we picked at our sandwiches. Syrie rubbed her plum against her shirt, told me that her older sister mentioned something about thieves, roving youths with enormous dogs. Syrie found it hard to believe any dog was dangerous; she'd only known kind breeds. I didn't know any. Perhaps it was the deep purple, but when Syrie bit the plum I expected blood to run down either side of her chin like the painted mouth of a marionette.

That night, in the dark, Syrie lights a book of matches. She holds it aloft like an offering. We pretend it's a torch. We pretend we're in a tomb.

The next day, one of Syrie's older sisters was leaning against the mailbox. She told me Syrie couldn't come out today, probably not tomorrow either. I asked why. Syrie's sister smiled like an actress and said, "It's just a little blood. You'll understand when you're older."

I spent the afternoon in my room listening to Otis Redding cassettes and ate two peanut butter and banana sandwiches.

Syrie was at her mailbox the next day, jaw set tight. At 435 Cañada she lay on the surf-blue bed for a while, "headachey." I pulled out the remaining ice cream and pretended I was Bruce Wayne. Syrie decided she would be Robinson Crusoe. We had dinner at Wayne Mansion, toured the Bat Cave, compared sidekicks.

With daylight left, we walked to Sacre Couer Blvd. At sunset, we rattled door handles. We decided on no. 36, because Syrie's favorite number was six and mine was three.

A door to the one-car garage was open, empty. Dust outlined the shape of a beach chair against a wooden wall. Syrie found a coat hanger in a plastic bag, picked the lock to the house. No. 36 Sacre Couer Blvd was a split-level, the bottom floor filled with a family history's worth of books, insurance forms, and diplomas. In the kitchen freezer Syrie and I found coffee grounds and took turns smelling. Two bikes leaned against one wall, left behind.

Home, sleep, dreams of dogs and the smell of pharmacies. The next morning, Syrie and I went to no. 36 and grabbed the bikes. We raced the mile to the bodega, where Syrie bought a bag of lemons. A flat mile back to no. 36, the bag of lemons hung from my handlebars, bumping my knee in a hurry to be sliced. In the kitchen, I crushed ice cubes with a hammer. We squeezed lemon juice over the ice and spooned sugar, sipped the drinks as they melted, stirring with our fingers, watching the sun drop oblong along the horizon like a lemon itself.

That night we sat on the pea-green couch and watched an old horror movie. Black and white teenagers screaming and kissing. We weren't scared, but we weren't bored either. When the movie ended, Syrie told me a story.

"There was a tiger once, when we were on vacation and my father was still around. Before Danielle had braces, but after Emily got the fishhook scar. We went to the shore, and I don't remember much about it. There were lots of low-houses and sand and only grass sticks out of the sand and grows high but looks lonely. Most of the trees are planted along the sidewalks, and it's obvious someone put them there. Those trees have little fences around their roots. But we were out on the dunes, and Mom says that's why the tiger was a problem. I could only go outside with her or my father, who was big and mean as a tiger anyway. Danielle and Emily could go out, but only together and only during the day. There were lifeguards along the beach with binoculars who had been given special training to watch for tigers as well as drowners and sharks. Danielle and Emily wore whistles around their necks."

I asked, "How did the lifeguards deal with the tiger?"

"Dune buggies and bikes. Then they would shoot the tiger with rifles. Maybe wrestle it. The parts I don't know, I'm making up. One night, the tiger was right by our beach house. I was asleep, but Mom said it almost ate Danielle. Thank god Dad overheard and stepped in. But even he couldn't kill it."

"I didn't know tigers lived by the beach," I said.

"There are tigers everywhere," said Syrie.

I suspected she meant something outside my experience. She spoke both to me and beyond me, but I could only blink in response, thinking of large cats. She fell silent, and then asleep. I listened for the tiger. But I only heard small noises outside the house. The proximity of tree branches to window panes, the sound of pebbles rolling over concrete.

We spent almost a week at Sacre Couer Blvd. Syrie disliked the tape collection and fetched the records from our house on Cañada. We rolled out sheets of butcher paper and drew maps of the neighborhood from memory, lying on the floor at diagonals, arms brushing. The maps intertwined, nonsensically, and from a distance looked like circuit boards. Syrie swept eraser dust from her arm and wondered aloud where eraser dust goes when it disappears on its own.

Syrie made the best map, but we disagreed on where to start the scouting expedition. Our disagreements were never sharp or mean. Syrie won, punching me lightly until I agreed. She thought she was coercing me, when in fact the feel of her knuckles and fingers were a gift, a small sampling of intimacy.

Syrie chose Ollie Lane because it only had one house. A tall house, narrow, painted green in the center of a pine copse. The tree branches lingered closely, blocked views from the first two floors. Syrie called the fourth floor The Tower.

We cleared no. 36 Sacre Couer of our presence, returned the records to 435 Cañada. That night, I listened to my parents whisper in the next room. I put my ear to their door, balanced myself against the creek of a floorboard. "They're kids," said my father. I felt the sad shake of my mother's head. "It's innocent," said my father. "And even if..." he began, but their voices trailed off to the far side of the room, became a soft purr.

Even if. These words kept me awake for hours. I was on the cusp of understanding something. I fell asleep counting the syllables, one-two-three.

The next morning, mom made me a sandwich with bacon. I ate half, wrapped the other half in paper towels, and stuck it in my pack with cereal, confectionary cake mix, and chocolate syrup. Syrie dumped the bread and ate the bacon as we walked to Ollie Lane, telling me about a TV show she'd watched with her sisters—something about high school, about a basketball player who is also a father. I picked up pebbles as we walked, ones large enough to reach high windows but small enough not to break glass. Walking with my head down, I nearly collided with Syrie. Through her shirt, I saw she was wearing a bathing suit, strap outlines right along her shoulder blades. Before I asked why, she sped up, still talking about TV.

We spent an hour throwing stones at the windows of Ollie Lane. We climbed each pine and peered into windows with yellow, plastic binoculars. No one was home. It was just objects, which Syrie read out from her notebook: antique rocking horse, porcelain salt and pepper shaker collection, boudoir of makeup. The skeleton key lock was easy to pick, but we forgot to lock it behind us. That night and the next.

Exploring the tall house: old tea leaves in tins, a box of cigars under a bottle of gin. The kitchen door lead into a red-brick walled garden. The second floor wall-papered white, a child's nursery. The third floor, books and bathrooms. Fourth, Syrie's tower, a master bedroom, paneled in wood, smelling like pines, pollen coating the windowsills like yellow snow. Syrie opened a window, wiped some pollen and sniffed it—a train of sneezes. I laughed, she shadow-boxed me, my stomach flipped.

The next day we went out earlier than usual. Our shoes got wet with dew walking to Ollie Lane. Syrie pulled off her sneakers, walked barefoot across pinecones, Jesus on water.

It was Syrie's idea to assemble a medicine chest—herbs, like a witch doctor's. She spent half an hour in the walled garden. I watched from an upstairs window, and when she came in, her nose and shoulders were sunburnt. The garden dried up in the heat, but Syrie had samples of dried and crumbling plant leaves in old nail polish bottles. She arranged them in a child's suitcase. The colors weren't all right though, and she filled a few bottles with food coloring, a few more with bluebells and evergreen berries. She called it a herbarium.

We found red candles and lit them at the kitchen table over squares of paper towel to keep wax from congealing on the wood. Syrie told more stories about the tiger—how it slept under the boardwalk and hunted in the surf by the abandoned piers. Or how the inland tigers stalked playgrounds and the fences at the edge of schoolyards. Tigers with cubs, and old tigers, scarred across their flanks and bellies.

I asked her if the stories were real. She considered this, then said they were made up, but with germs of hearsay or shore legend.

I was unsatisfied, but Syrie had gone stoic and distant.

"Tell me another," I said.

Syrie shrugged. She promised to ask Danielle more about the tiger.

Syrie yawned. "The Tower bed is an Eastern King," Syrie said.

We fell asleep there, and in the morning realized we'd forgotten to blow out the candles.

We'd left parents behind. We were the oldest people in our world. Syrie unpacked a backpack of peanut butter and chocolate. She had a tiny book, *A Barkeeper's Handbook*. She spent the afternoon reading it and that night made something called a gin fizz. I didn't drink much because it tasted awful. Syrie agreed, but drank a bit more. We were red in the face, flushed with one another. We ate the peanut butter and chocolate. We found more candles and set them at important points through the house, unlit. Lights off, we made a game of finding the candles in the dark, lighting them. Each time, the flame surprised us. Yellow tongue in Syrie's hand, a small fire in my chest.

Syrie went home for lunch the next day. I stared at the ceilings in Ollie Lane, all four of them. Long hours. When Syrie returned, I jump around her. She called me a puppy. Danielle had no more tiger stories, but warned us to be careful, since thieves had been broken into a house on Sacre Couer. Their dogs had killed a cat, left its body in the street. The poor cat. Despite this, we quickly forgot the thieves and dogs.

Syrie drank more gin fizz, put on the radio, and we danced. Not dancing exactly, but kicking our legs out, trying to make each other laugh. We fell asleep on the Eastern King, our lungs hurting. Syrie kissed me on the ear like a whisper.

I heard him first. He woke me up, trying to be silent, claws clicking and pausing, mid-stride, holding his tiger breath so I wouldn't smell it. A shade blocked the moonlight. I couldn't see the tiger but knew him by his stillness. Had I seen him before, out of the corners of my eyes? He came closer. I hoped that if he bit into me, it would be quick, it wouldn't wake Syrie. And being bitten, would I myself become a tiger—grow furred and feral?

But then: downstairs, a shattering, a glass gunshot. The tiger and I moved at once. He vanished, upsetting a children's stool that fell and rolled about the floor. Syrie was awake now, asking, "Is it the dogs?" More glass shattering, this time like raindrops, wind chimes. Syrie and I ran to the stairs, Syrie clutching her herbarium, swinging her backpack over a shoulder. In a clean line of moonlight from above, I see Syrie's lips, bright red from where she'd bitten them. There were growls from downstairs, then teenage voices: two or four or twelve of them and speaking all at once. Someone laughed. Another sharp shattering of glass, a chandelier crashing, but we didn't move. They were stomping in circles. Teenagers, older kids, students, maybe a whole classroom. Furniture tossed, plates smashed, water running.

Somewhere, a radio turned on, and immediately Otis Redding was singing. The world seemed snowy and dark, everything was black and white, black and moonlight. Syrie's hand on my arm hurt. Shadows on the stairs, like tall chess pieces, horse-faced, crowned by spiny hats. Syrie had been whispering, "Go, go, go, go, go, go, go, go," and her hand pressed me forward, down the stairs. I went, her behind me, heavy-pawed, ready to leap, to take a body down under my weight. But I was inelegant—stumbling and running as I barreled into the first body coming up the stairs. It went tumbling and I nearly tripped over something hairy as Otis Redding screamed, "I got dreams *bad dreams* dreams *rough dreams*..." Off the landing, I swung around a tight corner, through a doorway. I kept reaching back to assure myself Syrie was there, all the way out the front door, sneakers crunching broken glass, boys yelling, dogs barking, and thank god we fell asleep with our shoes on.

We ran until we were burning up, fire all through our legs and lungs and hearts. We ran what seemed like miles, eventually falling over in a copse of oak and pine in a back corner of the neighborhood. I recognized a boulder hugging an old elm and knew we were a few steps from Syrie's backyard. Syrie lied down in the pine needles. We caught our breath. I stood, impatient, pacing. But when Syrie reached out to touch my face, I could only say, "We're okay."

"You're bleeding," Syrie said, pointing to a corner of my thumb, where I'd grazed the broken glass door on the way out. A fine bubble of blood. She put her mouth to it and I closed my eyes. We fell asleep, holding one another tightly, and only woke the next morning when one of Syrie's sisters nudged me with the toe of her shoe. "Morning, tiger," she said with a smile. "You two get lucky?"

That was my last summer with Syrie. Her mom was forced to move into a smaller house across town. One sister went off to the college, soon the other, and it was too expensive to stay in the neighborhood. "All this space costs money," my mom reminded me.

Syrie fought it. You could hear her fight it from five houses down—at night, a strange keening. I liked to think she was crying for me. But for weeks before the move, Syrie ignored me. We passed silently on the sidewalk. She dodged my gestures like gunfire, like magic spells. I thought she was playing at first.

There were three neighborhood cases of arson reported that fall—a woodpile caught fire three houses down from Syrie's, then a lawnmower shed across the street, and finally a two-car garage, nearly gutted, at the end of one cul-de-sac. Stove matches and lighter fluid were left at each. Teenagers, their roving packs of dogs, probably. Who else? I imagined Syrie setting flame to wood, gingerly as she once placed the swollen petals of lady slippers into her herbarium. I wished I could be there with her.

Days before the move, a neighbor threw a Christmas party. Amid sweaters and slacks, Syrie and I were presented to one another like dancing partners. Tinsel ringed the snack table and Syrie held a reindeer-shaped sugar cookie in one hand. Her mom stood over her, a hand smoothing Syrie's hair as if she were years younger. "I know Syrie will miss you," said her mom.

"He'll be at loose ends next summer," my mom laughed, as if any of it were funny.

I later found her in the corner with a cup of Christmas punch. Syrie's remaining sister was drinking the eggnog and laughing too loud. I wanted to crawl under a table, like a much younger child. I wanted to pull Syrie with me.

What could I have said to her, my heart burning like the Christ's? What did I want from her? To be wedded, neatly as two rings? We skirted the edge of childhood. We would never walk barefoot and guileless again.

"Have you seen the tiger?" I asked.

"What tiger?" she said, looking away, as if for an escape.

I asked her to describe her new home, hoping for the corners and arches of our old houses, imagined and real. Story after story after story.

"Two bedrooms," said Syrie. "One bath."

She had the same zip code but a different telephone number, so Syrie said it wasn't worth calling. Then, because she knew she'd hurt me, she apologized. "Sorry. I'm a jerk tiger." As she said this, tears broke from her eyes, and I must have been crying too because my face was suddenly wet. It was time to go. Syrie put on her coat. She approached me, the uneaten cookie still in her hands. She gave it to me, then kissed me on the ear again, and my forehead, offering a blessing. Too old to be kissed on the forehead by anyone, too young to be kissed on the mouth.

The summers came and went and neighbors stopped going to the shore so much. "What with the economy and all…" they told my mother at the grocery store, the car wash. They stayed home late into the summer and could be seen tanning outside, reading books in the orchard, walking dogs.

Once I got my license, I borrowed my parent's car and went to the shore. There wasn't much there but sand and an ocean the color of bed sheets. I began walking.

I took off my shoes and socks and prowled the cool, wet sand by the water. Fat college envelopes had begun arriving. Too many for our mailbox, so the postman left them in neat piles on the font step.

There was a family down the strand and the ground grew pebbly, so I turned back. I could see the car in the lot a quarter mile away. The world had broadened recently, become larger and in doing so become strangely small and too familiar. How repetitious it all was—these streets, these stores and restaurants and parties.

After sitting for a while, I gathered my shoes and socks in one hand. I would go looking for animal prints in the dunes. I would only find my own.

Happening to Music

A Conversation with Matthew Rickart

The following conversation was conducted by senior fiction editor Dan Leach.

Dan Leach: Let's kick this thing off, yeah?

Matthew Rickart: That sounds great!

DL: Stories about childhood told in the retrospective first person POV can be complex on several levels. For one, you have to decide how much time has passed between the events of the story and the telling of the story. Moreover, once you determine that distance, you have to decide how much clarity and authority the speaker wields towards the past events. Can you talk a little bit about this process? When and where do you imagine your speaker to be as he remembers the events of that summer? And was that point in time fixed or did you move it in various drafts?

MR: I hugely enjoy stories told in retrospect that don't hold memory sacrosanct and acknowledge fallibility. Proust does this, as do dozens of excellent mystery novels. In my own fiction, I love showing the same scene from different character perspectives with small changes in dialogue, or re-ordering some of the action. Despite this, I like it when characters speak with absolute clarity—I think most of us do, since it makes for more compelling prose. And it's also how we tend to treat our own memories. Objectively, we know they're fallible, but they're also our story and narrative, so memories seem as absolute as events in a book, clearly paginated.

When it came to deciding how much time had passed between the narration and the events of "Fires," I didn't entirely know until I'd finished a few drafts. (In fact, earlier drafts were in the present tense, which is sort of my default.) Eventually, I settled on someone newly out of college. Still young, still a kid in many respects, but with that gulf of time between then and now. At twenty-two, he might just as well feel ninety. This is sort of Hollywood melodramatic, but I also imagine him recalling the story while standing on a beach. Not the same beach where he ends this story—but in a sense, all beaches are the same beach, right? Still, I don't think he's telling it aloud. I think he's just telling it to himself, sitting in the sand.

DL: I like what you said about the incident for retrospection being a beach and about how it's conceivable that this speaker is telling the story to himself. In fact, I think you establish this dynamic very early in the story in passages such as this one:

"We were kids. What games did we play? When other kids played with us, I only wanted to be on Syrie's team, her attention like warm light in November."

I love that you install that question between the two declarative thoughts. As a reader, you trust this speaker's recollection, not only because he is eloquent but even more so because he is clear. And yet, there are moments (such as this one), where he falters, second-guesses, grasps, admits ambiguity, or surrenders to mystery. My favorite moment in the story has this quality:

"What could I have said to her, my heart burning like the Christ's? What did I want from her? To be wedded, neatly as two rings? We skirted the edge of childhood. We would never walk barefoot and guileless again."

I wonder if you view this story, in certain sense, as a story about memory. About what you can know looking back (and all the vivid details rendered from that knowing), but also what you cannot know, what you must wonder about as you stand on a beach years removed? I've gone on much too long in asking this question, but only because I love this story so much and was so deeply moved by moments such as these. I guess what I'm really asking is for you to talk a bit about how memory is dealt with in the story. You might discuss the passages above but also the tone in general (which feels haunted, right?).

MR: I think it's a story about memory in the sense that it's a story about longing, both for another person and for another self. Those two passages you cite have a lot of questions in them, but they're kind of rhetorical, I think. I'm not sure he's really interrogating these memories so much as trying to live in them. He asks the questions to recall the unknowns rather than to try to find an answer.

And I would definitely say the tone feels haunted at times. That's what I was going for, at least! But I think it's a sort of daytime haunting. It's not insidious or actively dangerous—certainly not spooky. I think it's haunted the way any home movies feel vaguely haunted. It all borders on the sentimental, too.

I like that famous bit of dialogue from The Glass Menagerie that goes, "The play is memory. Being a memory play, it is dimly lighted, it is sentimental, it is not realistic. In memory everything seems to happen to music." I tried applying some of this aesthetic to "Fires."

DL: If your goal was to create a world where "everything seems to happen to music," I think you hit your mark. In fact, one of the first things that our editorial staff remarked on was the cadence and sonic quality of your sentences. I'll ask you this because (as a writer) it's the question I always wish someone would ask me. What are some (let's say three) of your favorite sentences? And, if you wouldn't mind, could you say what it is you like about these sentences?

MR: Oh boy. My three favorite sentences I've ever read?

1. "All the world's a stage we're going through."

This is from Lorrie Moore's novel *Anagrams*. But I could pick three sentences and they'd all be Lorrie Moore probably. (Runner up: "This danish is too sweetish to finish.") Anyway, I love this sentence for all the obvious reasons: it's clever, also actually funny, and it just reads well even though it shouldn't. The way that "All the world's a..." joins with "we're going through" via the playful double-meaning of "stage" is just so satisfying. And the sentence is surprising—it doesn't end where you expect! It reminds me of when a song's verse just dovetails right into its chorus.

2. "Love must wait; it must break one's bones."

If "favorite sentences" is really just "sentences you've had stuck in your head since you read them," this one applies. It's from James Salter's novel *Light Years*, a book I return to often. And yeah, a bit dour compared to Moore. My love of this sentence is complicated. I love its certainty, and the way it fits that absolutism into two clauses within one sentence. But I also recognize that declarative, mid-century male-writer prose is potentially played out. I like to think there's an uncertainty and anxiety underlying it, the way I think these underlie so much in *Light Years*.

3. "On the sliding-door cabinet (we have turned the corner now and are moving toward the windows) there is a pottery lamp with a wide perforated grey paper shade and such a long thin neck that it seems to be trying to turn into a crane."

I'm showing my sentimental side, but I love this particular sentence from William Maxwell's short story "The Thistles in Sweden." The story itself is a plotless, loosely-constructed sort-of-memoir. The narrator and his wife live in a NYC apartment in the 1950s, and he spends pages taking us on a tour of that small apartment. Rather than being mundane (much less boring), it's an entrancing and soothing little adventure. This sentence is emblematic of all of that: the ways in which it interrupts itself parenthetically, using "we" to bring you in, so make you a guest. The simple, literal description of the lamp. And then the beautiful surprise of that closing, in which lamp is made bird. Maxwell gives the lamp itself agency (it is trying to "turn itself"), and there's a sweetness in this I love.

Now that I've rambled on for so long... I'm curious what some of yours are!

DL: Such great answers. Such great sentences. I wish Salter got more attention than he does, as he is certainly one of the great sentence writers of the past century. You asked about mine? I don't know. Sentences, for me, are kind of like songs. The ones that cut you deepest did so when you were young and impressionable. Does that make sense? In other words, it's hard to argue that Bush is a better band than The Hold Steady; but "Everything Zen" sure did cut my fourteen-year old soul in a way that The Hold Steady probably can't manage with my thirty-five year old soul, callused as it is. So with respect to sentences, I really go back to the ones that got me in my early twenties, when I was first starting to write fiction. Fred Exley has some real heartbreakers in *A Fan's Notes.* Updike in *Rabbit, Run*, but also in so much of his short fiction. I like this one from Barry Hannah so much I memorized it: "The point is to strip down, get protestant, then even more naked. Walk over scorched bricks to find your own soul. Your heart a searching dog in the rubble." That's from what I think is his worst book, *Yonder Stands Your Orphan.* Of course the late Toni Morrison had so many great ones, too.

Let me switch gears here from sentence-level stuff to larger structural concerns. With respect to setting, it always feels good to ground a story about childhood in summer. But what I love about the summer in "Setting of Small Fires" is its connection with departures. The opening paragraph has that great line about Syrie and the speaker watching the neighborhood "vacate itself." This seems like such a crucial decision in terms of its symbolic implications and emotional resonances but also in terms of what it allows the kids to do. Can you talk a little bit about how you see emptiness and departures functioning in the story?

MR: I always like those apocryphal statements about how the music we listen to in high school or college determines our taste throughout the rest of our life. (Partially, I just like the idea that someone out there might have chosen this as a course of study.) But I totally agree. I sometimes wonder if anything will move me as much as that line about spilling apple juice in Blink-182's "Adam's Song" did at thirteen.

I have a notebook somewhere full of transcribed sentences from *Rabbit, Run.* And I deeply love his short story "The Happiest I've Been." I also find myself thinking of Toni Morrison in the present tense still. *The Bluest Eye* was the first of hers I read, and it's the one I return to most. There's something I'm really struggling to define about not just her sentences but storytelling that is so intensely personal and memorable. They get under your skin and in your psyche. Especially *Bluest Eye* for me because of its focus on childhood and adolescence.

Which dovetails nicely with talking about "Fires"! The emptiness of the neighborhood is crucial to the plot and to the fantasy of living in other people's homes for an afternoon—but it also reflects this dual experience of childhood to me. On the one hand, as kids, we're often oblivious to adults. We experience time differently, we're less beholden to it. Same with responsibility. As a kid, it's sometimes difficult to escape daydreams or your own imagination. So I think of the empty neighborhood as a reflection of my own experiences growing up, when my friends and I would run through yards and fields—property our parents didn't own—in sprawling games of tag.

On the other hand, I think it's also about the hyper-awareness of being left alone. Because while children are often oblivious to adults, they're almost intuitively keyed into adult presence and absence. I think of the first time I was left home alone (just a little younger than the narrator, probably) and the intense freedom of having a house to myself. A house I knew inside-and-out, but which was suddenly transformed. I'm pretty sure the thrill of independence was in competition with a lingering fear of ghosts.

DL: So since you've been hitting homeruns on all these other tough questions, let me throw one more curveball. In your last response you talked about how the setting (particularly an empty town) collaborates with the story's psychology (being a kid and, more specifically, being left alone). This, for me, is one of the most impressive effects an author can achieve. John Updike, who we've already mentioned, is a master. As is Stuart Dybek and many Southern authors such as Eudora Welty and Ron Rash. Here's my question, though: how did you stage this collaboration? In other words, what came first—the kid who feels left behind or a town that left? Did you start with the vacated setting and populate it with a kid who felt, naturally, lonely? Or did you start with a kid who felt lonely then realize that a vacated town would amplify (and even symbolize) this loneliness?

MR: This story had its first draft in 2010, so some of my memory is a little fuzzy. I believe the empty neighborhood/town came first, and then Syrie came second. I had just graduated undergrad and moved home for a season, so I was surrounded by the landscape of my childhood: trees climbed, hills raced over, etc. I wanted to capture that feeling of expansiveness, but also the diminishing of it. The way that age takes that from you. And through Syrie I tried to express the intensity of childhood friends, regardless of gender, and how those friendships change irrevocably, usually when the confusion of sex and attraction gets layered on.

I think the loneliness is more a byproduct of all of that. And that for writers loneliness can sometimes be a default state.

DL: "Loneliness as default." I love that. And it's true. Well, since my last few questions have been somewhat rigid in terms of my directing you to one specific craft issue, let me hit you with a few open-ended ones.

What is an image in the story (or, for that matter a symbol or a moment or a sentence) that readers might be tempted to underestimate? What, without giving away too much, makes this thing so important within the larger context of the story?

MR: That's a tough one, since every reader locks into a story in different ways, if at all! Hard to know what someone might underestimate.

I guess I'd choose the line, "Too old to be kissed on the forehead by anyone, too young to be kissed on the mouth." I think that's a particular experience. When you don't want to be seen as a child, and you both daydream about and are a little intimidated by adolescence. You're in this nebulous space between two stages of life. And it feels long, even when it might only last a summer. I wanted to articulate that.

DL: Quote a piece of writing advice that guides your process.

MR: Write if it's compulsive or it brings you joy. Otherwise, I don't recommend it.

DL: Quote a piece of writing advice you actively disregard in your process.

MR: People say it's important to create a writing routine, but few of us have the luxury of routine. I write where and when I can. One trick: arrive twenty minutes early for everything and bring a notebook. Also, maybe turn off your phone.

DL: Where can readers find more of your work, and what are you working on now?

MR: I've published a few short stories. Most recently, the story "Palms & Palms" in the Fall 2018 volume of *The Madison Review.*

I'm revising one novel and drafting a new one. Weirdly, this is my natural state—juggling multiple novels.

DL: Okay, Matt, well as we wrap up, is there anything else you'd like to add?

MR: Hmm. I'm not sure I have anything profound to say. I suppose: despite all the cat and tiger stuff, I'm really more of a dog person.

"KNOCKED OUT"

"POOL PARTY"

“BEAUTY GURU”

“CAT PATIO”

AFTERLIFE OF A DUMPED BODY

ANNIE CIGIC

A tightly wrapped body made
into an aviary: a dead place kept
for captives. It threatened
pleasure—to take away a sweet sweat
quivering in the neck's nape, unguided
in the dip of its back. The lungs asked why
the body chooses sheer drops to fall
to death—like it's an obsession
with the unambiguous—
reclaiming an unknown part of the earth
met at impact, asking to eat
a corner of the river away.
A river's wholeness can't be swiped
by the body's drought—emptied
of melodies. No, this body is full
with blame: *know better*. Why burn
a constructed shame?
Where silence crawls, the body
can only birth a mouth full
of cotton, its cherried heart runs
out of seeds, & the burgundy-marbled
skin, left there, melts
in the snow. Some tenderness asked
for, but spirits strap themselves to the body—
a type of darkness that guts faith
                    guts a good memory
                    guts the sky
                    guts shock
                    guts innocence
                    guts a mother's cry
                    guts permission
                    guts absence into its being.
Now would be the time for God
to be real.

INTERVIEW
WITH ANNIE CIGIC

What inspired the poem?

"Afterlife of a Dumped Body" is actually inspired by a few things. It started with the painting *The Lovers* by René Magritte. I wrote a poem in response to that painting, then another poem in response to that poem. They were both short poems. "Afterlife of a Dumped Body" was inspired by those two shorter poems and the TV shows I'd been watching: *Twin Peaks* and *The Keepers* on Netflix. News platforms at the time were covering a story of a missing girl, which also had a huge impact on this poem.

What was the hardest part about writing it?

I think trying to convey a mother's grief and understanding the concept of an afterlife and applying those to the poem were difficult.

What came easiest when writing this poem?

Surprisingly, the form and title. I started out with the form it is in now and it just seemed to work and come naturally to me when I wrote the very first draft.

How much revision went into this poem?

Most of the revisions I made focused on the sentences and word choices. The first draft had inconsistent and awkward syntax. Some of the word choices didn't hit as hard or added confusion. For lines that were choppy and unclear, I added more detail so the images in the poem would become more visceral.

Is this poem categorical of your work? Why or why not?

Yes and no. I say yes because of its weird and surreal moments and the tone. I say no because my poems are usually shorter, in couplets, and don't address religion. "Afterlife of a Dumped Body" is also more lyrical than some of my other poems.

What is your favorite line from the poem or the line you are most proud of?

The very last line is probably what I'm most proud of, but my personal favorite line is, "Where silence crawls, the body / can only birth a mouth full / of cotton, its cherried heart runs / out of seeds, & the burgundy-marbled / skin, left there, melts / in the snow."

Is there anything unique about your personal writing process?

A huge part of my writing process actually takes place in my head. I've had lines and words stay in my head for as long as six months before I write them down. I work out a lot of ideas in my head first, then I usually type it into my phone or on a piece of paper that's by me. I'm not sure how or when I decide to transfer the ideas in my head to paper, but it seems like a spontaneous moment. I think I'll need to get in the habit of writing down lines immediately just in case I forget them in the future.

How long do you usually spend working on a single poem?

It varies! Sometimes I write a poem in under an hour and it's done, or I spend months working on a single poem.

How long have you been writing poetry? What has changed from your first poem to your newest work?

I have been writing poetry for fourteen years. I

can't say I've been consistent with it during those fourteen years though. Just within the past year I've found my voice and writing style. Subject manner, tone, form, etc. all changed since I wrote my first poem. I used to write poems for people, but I don't do that as often now. My poems are more lyrical and surreal now, and they focus a lot on trauma, my subconscious mind, grief, and shame.

Who are some of your favorite poets?

Some of my favorites are Julie Doxsee, Maggie Smith, Jericho Brown, T.S. Eliot, Leila Chatti, Traci Brimhall, Ross Gay, Melissa Cundieff, Natalie Shapero, Anne Sexton, Sylvia Plath, Ada Limón, etc.

How would you personally define poetry?

Poetry can be defined in numerous ways, so I find this to be a difficult question. But for me, poetry is an art form that not only functions line-by-line but also deals in words. Poetry utilizes space to create certain effects, like breathlessness. I think poetry carries a lot of weight and stakes and makes you wonder about and question life. It helps you view experiences from different perspectives, and we need poetry to look for meaning beyond our worlds and trauma. There's a lot that poetry is and a lot that poetry does, but sometimes it fills in the spaces for us and we can apply it to our own life experiences.

Based on your personal experience, what advice would you give to other writers?

Trust yourself. Don't apologize for your poems. Rejection is part of the process, so don't stop trying to find a "home" for your work, even if it has been rejected more than a handful of times. Listen to feedback carefully. Do your best in revision, but don't revise forever. It's okay if you have to distance yourself from a piece and it's okay to not write every single day. Either way, know that you are doing meaningful work and your voice has a place in our world.

Where can readers find more of your work?

Gordon Square Review, Havik, Bookends Review, Silver Needle Press, and *The Hunger.*

What drew you to *Driftwood Press*?

First, I absolutely loved the layout of the website. It's easily accessible and the work is beautiful. *Driftwood Press* publishes a lot of wonderful writers, a wide variety of genres, and they care about creative work in general and promoting and celebrating their contributors. It's a great place to find the best of poetry, fiction, comics, visual art, etc. I'm really excited to be included!

EXISTENCE: SEVEN LEVELS

JIWON CHOI

samurai

on the razor's edge
your spine must be
the sword

metaphor

heads
in a sack
each one a bloody
exclamation
punctuating your
exultation

politico

jesus
had a plan
that went viral

what have you got?

girls in half shirts
tweeting
at half time

artifact

night at the museum
is
firm buttocks
rouged lips
sharpened teeth
is
pygmy

behind glass

dogma

in sinatra's swan song
eternity is played by
ernest borgnine who stops
and frisks all the army
scenes:

you won't box?
then I'll put you
in one

classic prima dogma
syndrome

death

bloated sewers
and dead bodies
on subway
platforms

you know
the water has
nowhere to go

poet

henry dumas rifles
through our icebox
looking for that last drop
of cream for coffee

who's going to tell him
ghosts can't drink?

INTERVIEW
WITH JIWON CHOI

What inspired the poem?

I had recently watched *Ghost Dog*, which I'd never seen and was inspired to write the poem as homage to the wayward warrior (aka hit man) played by Forest Whitaker. I was taken with the character and his journey through the inner and outer realms of his psyche, as he tries to make sense and work out the laws of honor and ethics he's created for himself.

How much revision went into this poem?

I started this poem in 2014 and it has maintained much of its original structure in spite of my wanting the stanzas to be on the sparser side. There was a fair amount of whittling down and at times I wondered if it was cutting too much. This question of "when is it done?" is the eternal question. How to answer? There is no magic formula to know, but as a poet you'll have to access the part of you that knows when to stop.

Is this poem categorical of your work? Why or why not?

I felt at the time that I was writing a poem that was different than what I had been creating. And that was a wonderful feeling. This poem was the hardest to place, consistently getting rejected, but the rejections just made me want to support it more. And though the structure of the piece with its stanza headings is not how I usually construct my work, I think the point of writing is that you find new ways of expressing yourself. Don't turn on the autopilot mode: surprise yourself. Surprise your readers.

What is your favorite line from the poem or the line you are most proud of?

I like ending the poem with the presence of Henry Dumas, a poet whose life and career were cut short when he was killed by NYC transit police. The idea that there could be a poet ghost like Dumas in my kitchen is exciting.

Who are some of your favorite poets?

I am very impressed by the work of Philip Levine and am guided by the integrity and value of his poetry. He was the poet of the working class as he himself worked hard jobs before becoming a professor. I am currently finishing his collection of essays, published posthumously, and learning so much from him still.

And it's good to read poets who are still alive and writing, and the three I have been consistently admiring and reading are Yusef Komunyakaa, Naomi Shihab-Nye, and Bob Hershon.

How would you personally define poetry?

I believe in poetry and I think it's an art form that is embedded in everything in our lives. It is a force for good and as poets we are responsible for keeping it relevant and accessible to the larger public. Also, I want to remind everyone that writing is not for a special segment of the population, it is for all of us. It's important for us poets and writers to encourage each other and others to take up the task of writing and connecting to humanity-at-large through our shared experience and insights.

Where can readers find more of your work?

I have a first book of poetry, *One Daughter is Worth Ten Sons*, published by *Hanging Loose Press* that readers can check out. And my work can also be found on *Rigorous* (online) and in *Hanging Loose Magazine* (print). I have an interview on *Palette Poetry* and an upcoming essay on emerging writers on *Frontier Poetry*. I also edit poetry for *Typehouse Literary Magazine*, so even though the poems are not mine, you can get a sense of the work I admire.

PRAYER

KATHLEEN RADIGAN

My mother won't read
the oncology report.

Walks the dog by the sea. Drives for hours
under a bruised sky
and returns
with vanilla ice cream.

On my bed, she lays out
a corduroy skirt for church,
where stained glass
tints us pink.

PLEA TO GOD

KATHLEEN RADIGAN

Before You knock me up, let me birth fistfuls of gold moths.
Water snakes. Let ants dance out my mouth.
I'm only fourteen. I haven't felt a lot. I want sisters who are lizards.
Peer inside my belly full of animals: a circus, three thousand evolutionary years

I'll die a good virgin. I'll lie on him when it rains inside.
I'll lick his wounds, lock my knees, shelter him in spine.

Prophets say he's destined for a salt grave. I'll water his bones with tears.
But first I want gardens. Moony daughters whose braces collect sun.
A pool of your saliva as an emblem.

INTERVIEW

WITH KATHLEEN RADIGAN

What inspired the poem?

When I was a kid in Catholic kindergarten, I was terrified that I'd be picked to bear God's next son. I'm interested in how Mary had to sacrifice her own adulthood to serve a divine plan. I imagined her as a precocious teenager, asking for the chance to bear other things too, to be other people, before becoming an instrument for this larger narrative.

Is this poem categorical of your work? Why or why not?

A lot of my poetry is similar to these poems in that it's concerned with women, religion, and frustration. Also, I tend to write very weird image-based poems.

Who are some of your favorite poets?

Lately, I love Thomas James, Heather Christle, Rita Dove, Dorothea Lasky, Terrence Hayes, Tracy K Smith, and Frederico Garcia Lorca.

If you had to narrow it down, what three books have had the most impact on your writing?

The Unabridged Journals of Sylvia Plath, Mary Karr's *The Liar's Club,* and Alice Munro's *Hateship Loveship Courtship Friendship Marriage.*

Do you work in any other artistic mediums? If so, how do those other genres inform your poetry?

I love writing songs, singing, comedy, and puppetry. I gravitate toward mediums that allow me tell stories non-chronologically, and I love rubbing words together to create music.

How would you personally define poetry?

Charting the weird patterns of the mind.

Where can readers find more of your work?

My poems have been published in *Carve Magazine, the Academy of American Poets, New Ohio Review, The Adroit Journal, apt, The Antigonish Review,* and several other places.

NECKS, US

SAM STOKLEY

1. A slug will cross the earth if it means avoiding the salt wall between him and a green leaf.
2. In sixth grade I tried to keep a smile stifled while I read to the class my story—a puppy ecstatic during the bustle of an approaching twister.
3. The quickest way to ruin a dog is to punish it for the praxis praised as a puppy.
4. The essay writing score was my worst GRE result.
5. It's important to avoid valleys in roofing design—places where rain, ice and other weather settle.
6. You will find most leaks occur in valleys.
7. "Scalloped" is the technical term for the way a tongue looks when it's been wedged in closed-mouth teeth for hours.
8. Scallops are shellfish prized for their buttery flesh.
9. A canker sore mined its way through too much of my tongue before I could slow it.
10. Look, you can see the chunk it took, like punishment for some medieval crime.
11. The best way I know to remove a knot is to dig my fingers into the muscle until I feel a release.
12. With canker sores I follow a similar philosophy by putting a fresh, unlit match on the tongue's affected area, pressing for longer than I can stand until I could stand it forever.
13. Unlike a knot, cankers persist, but there's a release.
14. Is the hotdog lodged in your trachea or esophagus? The former, fatal; the other inconvenient, so relax.
15. There's always a release.
16. Animals will sacrifice their parts to save their whole but sometimes it's an overreaction and not a powerful metaphor.
17. You gonna eat that?
18. Unlike animals that imprint on the first being they see, sea turtles imprint on bodies of water.
19. You can keep a turtle away from water until old age and the moment it sees the ocean its life begins again.
20. Galapagos tortoises live for more than 100 years because they have a terrible sense of direction and it often takes decades to find the way.
21. Yes, giraffes have black tongues sitting upon miraculous necks, but it's the way they knob-knee themselves down to water or the lowest grass that's most awesome.
22. Miracles can be inconvenient.
23. Saliva and spearmint are my tongue's only memories from the month I poured liquid manna into a tube punched through my abdomen. The hole in my throat scarred over, and I haven't trusted my neck since.
24. The slug is in no rush.

INTERVIEW
WITH SAM STOKLEY

What inspired the poem?

Credit goes to my friend and fellow writer Rupa Thadhani who challenged me a few years back to write something about "why I write." I'd taken a circuitous path to writing, forcing myself away from it when I was younger before returning to it as a sophomore in college, so I tried to understand the motivations that led to my personal timeline.

What was the hardest part about writing it?

Truthfully, the title. For about half a year the poem sat with the title "The Way" before I took it to a *Tin House* workshop with Kevin Young and so many amazing writing peers. When I left the workshop the new title was "Scalloped," which lasted maybe a month before I changed it again to "Animal Praxis," which stuck for at least a year. Finally, earlier this year, the poem became "Necks, Us." I haven't had a desire to change it since, so I think we're good.

What came easiest when writing this poem?

The poem, frankly, not to be sassy. In its first handwritten form, the poem already was numbered with every major idea that appears in the final. After the slug idea lightbulbed, the next moments flowed one after another, maybe because the original kernel from Rupa about "why I write" is something I'd wondered myself for some time.

How much revision went into this poem?

Mostly syntax and organization. I think my first draft was maybe nineteen bullets, and after a couple years I adjusted the order and split some numbers up to get me to twenty-four, which felt fitting.

What is your favorite line from the poem or the line you are most proud of?

"22. Miracles can be inconvenient." When I tore my esophagus I remember two older ladies coming into my hospital room and laying hands on me, praying over me. I remember them praying "for a miracle," and I remember thinking, "I sure hope I don't need a miracle; I didn't think it was that serious." Sometimes I think we go so far out of our way to hope for a miracle when just the normal physics of reality would suffice. Miracles have an amazing ability to complicate things.

How long do you usually spend working on a single poem?

I don't think I can give a concise answer to this. Sometimes I will hand write a draft in a single day, put it on the computer the next day, and a "final" draft isn't far behind before I try to send it out to a couple places. But my notebook is 80% lines and half baked poems that might take (and have taken) years to coalesce into a complete poem. I like when it's the former, but most often it's the latter, so I'll say between three days and three years.

How long have you been writing poetry? What has changed from your first poem to your newest work?

In terms of my whole writing career, poetry is still new. For nearly eight years I wrote fiction and fiction only, mostly flash. I began my MFA program with fiction. It wasn't until Deborah Keenan, beloved mentor and writer, gave poem writing assignments and encouraged my results that I began exploring poetry in earnest. That was about three, almost four years ago.

The longer I live inside poetry, the further my work leaves behind the narrative and syntactical clarity of my fiction writing.

Who are some of your favorite poets?

To be real, my favorite poets are my friends who consistently impress and inspire me—poets like Emily Oliver, JD Hegarty, Chavonn Williams Shen, and Jen Manthey. But to select outside of my immediate circle, some writers I return to again and again are Tyehimba Jess, Gwendolyn Brooks, Inger Christensen, Jericho Brown, and Sun Yung Shin.

If you had to narrow it down, what three books have had the most impact on your writing?

Edgar Lee Masters' *Spoon River Anthology* is the only poetry I can remember reading (outside of Billy Shakes) up until college. In the end, it's just a book of gossip and receipts, so I think it's due for a resurgence. Tyehimba Jess' *Olio* is beyond any written description; its masterful weaving of narrative and character with formal and linguistic experimentation, up against cultural realities, continues to speak to both the fiction writer and poet inside me. Lastly, I'll go with Inger Christensen's *Alphabet* as translated by Susanna Nied. I just want the first seven or so sections (if not the whole book) tattooed on my body.

When someone pulls your ankles toward them at the foot of the bed and cups you like water to drink. You are about to be born once more,
twice more,
three times more,
twisted and trembling.

Knees that ache when the weather makes them and knees which fold when you make them.
To pew, to mourn, to honor, to reach, to suckle, to determine,
to set and reset,
to rise and be risen.

That popping you hear when you get back up is the same popping all the women in your family have ever heard
and it is the question being raised
what happens to our knees after they are no longer useful.

Is, perhaps, the end of me at my knee.

Before me, I hear women wail, *Where are you taking my knees, my baby's knees, only to the Basilica, please,*

and who is this holy You that people must answer to.

Have you ever heard your knees knock against someone else's? This is called the unavoidable kiss.

I will allow You to donate my knees only to the cathedrals Of My Choice so those without proper bones may lean down on borrowed kneecaps to feel whole again. This is called fair.

Knees knocking, knees bumping, knees kneading the bread—something warm and holy.
Pushing its yeast and the body and the skin, the trinity, pampering the places that will fold for us, may you forever escape the places that don't. Make the beginning meet the end, smooth two bookend places together so they feel like one.

You stretched your knees further than mine in order to help me.

This is all anyone can ask of another person. All anyone can do, for anyone else, ever. The absolute best thing.

INTERVIEW
WITH TAYLOR IMEL

What inspired the poem?

The death of my grandmother and a reoccurring knee injury. Both at the beginning of 2018, when I was scheduled to graduate college.

What came easiest when writing this poem?

The rhythm.

Was there anything in your original concept that did not make it in?

This is one poem that really came out in one go. I like to say what I need in the way I need, then revisit the piece or excerpt later for edits. This one had little revision. It came out almost exactly that way.

Is this poem categorical of your work? Why or why not?

This piece is more true-to-self than some older works. Pushing forward, I'm really questioning everything. I question what I like to do and how it relates to what I'm trying to say. This has brought me to photography and fiction writing and mixed-genre work, which are all places I never thought I would go. Ever. But I've always been curious and I've always questioned things. In college, I had things whirling around in my mind and I was never sure how to construct thought in a way that felt honest. It always felt like pleasing someone else or working toward satisfaction or wins. 2018 was incredibly sobering and it made me very conscious of if I'm staying honest.

What is your favorite line from the poem or the line you are most proud of?

"Knees that ache when the weather makes them and knees which fold when you make them."

It's nothing spectacular to me, but it is an homage to my grandmother, who was also an artist and a best friend. We talked about knees quite a bit. The bigger picture of all of this (what "Knees" is an excerpt from) is for her.

Is there anything unique about your personal writing process?

So I mainly write about my family. One of the "funniest" parts is the ethical consultation I have with myself every time I write something nonfiction-esq. Most of these conversations have happened with my mom. I'll write something about her, I'll submit it, it gets picked up, and I call her. She's not always enthused it's about her.

But my mom isn't a spotlight kind of person, and I think she's so fascinating. Like flowers at Alcatraz kind of cool. So every time I write about her, I make it part of my process to let her know I've written about her. I let her know it's because I find her incredible.

So far, I've only had to have this conversation with my mother. It's a personal choice, I've spoken to many nonfiction writers about how they do or do not go about letting their loved ones know they're in their stories. It really depends on the nature of the relationship and the writer's perspective.

How long do you usually spend working on a single poem?

Not long, initially! I like to get it all out in one go. The door is always open to go back and edit, though. I had an art teacher in high school (the late and great Joe Haft) explain it like this: "I'll finish a work, hang it in my hallway, and take it down every once in a while when I feel like I can make it better. I have a piece from ten years ago I still edit."

Who are some of your favorite poets?

I look to cross-genre writers. Adrianna Gonzalez's essay titled 'Sights of Narrowleaf Milkweed" is still on my mind; I read it months ago.

If you had to narrow it down, what three books have had the most impact on your writing?

Nox by Anne Carson—the most solid thing my writing professors in college suggested to me. *The People of Paper* by Salvador Placencia and Joan Didion's *The Year of Magical Thinking.*

Do you work in any other artistic mediums? If so, how do those other genres inform your poetry?

I've been working with photography for almost two years. In the beginning I was into disposable cameras. This project/manuscript that "Knees" is from is working to turn my photography and my writing into one told story. The story in itself involves a journey with paper, with identity, with image, with found objects and photos and conversations. It seemed fitting to use both mediums to tell a story that is still unraveling. It all gets me very excited.

How would you personally define poetry?

Thoughtettes.

Based on your personal experience, what advice would you give to other writers?

Everything you need is inside of you or on its way.

Where can readers find more of your work?

Hypertrophic Press, Into the Void, & *Zoetic Press*! Also on my instagram (@tayimel), where I post photo projects and life continuations, or my Wordpress page (taylorkimel.wordpress.com).

What drew you to *Driftwood Press*?

I was reading through a list of rated small presses and then browsed an online issue. I was thoroughly impressed from the go. So happy and so thankful to be with you artists.

& Porfirio Méndez Crosses into Manitoba

Daniel Aristi

Los Rojos
Que vienen los Rojos, the Reds
The Reds are coming, los Mounties, escóndanse, hide.
Hide under this snow, mother—think Moon dust, mother.
Escóndase bajo la nieve ésta, madre—Usted piense que es
Polvo de Luna, madre. It's harder
For us because we're made the color & heat of sun-bled sand
& this border crossing is for gringos. Nos es más difícil
Porque somos del color & del calor
De la arena que sangra el Sol & y esta frontera
Es para gringos.
We are the two-frontier tribe, somos la tribu de los pobres
Dos Fronteras:
Maple syrup on tortillas
En las tortillas, jarabe de arce
& Guacamole hard like jade
& Guacamole duro como el jade
& No fur in the sombrero
& El sombrero, sin pelaje
& Putting on three ponchos
& Poniéndose tres ponchos
& Jesus too bare on his silver cross—too cold
For miracles. & Jesús demasiado desnudo en su cruz de plata—
Demasiado frío para milagros.

INTERVIEW
WITH DANIEL ARISTI

What inspired the poem?

The situation of Hispanic migrants in the US in the recent past is the background against which the poem came about. The notion formed that maybe the Promised Land lays no more in the US but in Canada, and thus the States became then another country of passage in the travelers' long trek northwards. This, finally, brought about "La Tribu Dos Fronteras," those compelled to cross the two land borders of the United States in search of refuge. The subsequent contrasting imagery between warm and cold climates, between sand and snow and their ethnic extrapolations make the poem.

What came easiest when writing this poem?

Weaving English and Spanish, something I do often when writing poetry, came particularly easily in "Porfirio," especially in the last third of the piece where short sentences appear one after the other alternating languages in a rhythmic, one-two way that I enjoyed very much developing: "Maple syrup on tortillas / En las tortillas, jarabe de arce / & Guacamole hard like jade / & Guacamole duro como el jade / & No fur in the sombrero (…)"

Is there anything unique about your personal writing process?

I don't think there is anything unique about my writing process per se. Rather, it is the very roots of my writing poetry that are probably different having started learning English when I was fourteen—and I'm still at it, believe me—compounded by the fact that I look at the US from afar, very much an outsider. These two factors are bound to define my writing way before I put pen to paper.

How long do you usually spend working on a single poem?

I'd say two to three weeks to get the basic layout of it, at 75%, and then several months to get the other 25% right—which normally includes working on a decent ending, the most difficult bit. I used to be too impatient so I'd send poems out that were not fully polished and they obviously got rejected a bunch of times, so I'd bring them back home after a while, all bruised and bloodied, and I'd sit and refit them properly before submitting them again.

How long have you been writing poetry? What has changed from your first poem to your newest work?

About ten years now. I read those first poems and they're so bad it's laughable—"daba palos de ciego," as we say in Spanish, meaning I was like a blind person hitting around with a cane trying to find his way through darkness… I think my current work is more assertive, takes more risks, and builds on more original ideas. But I'm still searching for a voice I can confidently call mine, and I'm a million miles away from having a proper command of the English language.

Where can readers find more of your work?

There's quite a bit online and, poetry-wise, I'm grateful for having been recently published by *great weather for MEDIA* (in their latest anthology *Birds Fall Silent in the Mechanical Sea*), *Salt Hill Journal*, and *Main Street Rag*. Regarding short stories, which I also work on, one of my favorite flash fiction pieces is in *The Best Small Fictions 2016*.

THE NEXT DAY.

HARRIET HEYDEMANN

Gary moves your shower seat, bi-pap machines, feeding pump, suction devices, and pulse oximeter out of your bedroom, into the garage. He doesn't want to see the medical equipment. He doesn't want to be reminded of the medical you.

Three times we expanded the footprint of our house to add space and storage, as your ailments multiplied. Medical equipment here and here and here. An exercise ball too large for a closet. A suction device left out for immediate use. Every room said, "A person with a disability lives here."

Everything will go to my brother's clinic in Juarez.

"Leave the chair," I yell as he rolls it outside. Dried acrylics adorn the armrests. Blues overlay reds, overlay oranges, overlay greens.

He obliges but moves it to a corner.

INTERVIEW
WITH HARRIET HEYDEMANN

What inspired the poem?

The life and untimely death of my twenty-six year old daughter. She inspires much of my writing. She's sitting beside me as I type this.

What was the hardest part about writing it?

Reality is hard. A poem can't capture a whole complicated life story. This poem only gives the reader one small sliver of a story.

What came easiest when writing this poem?

Nothing. Writing poetry isn't easy for me.

Was there anything in your original conception that did not make it in?

Too much to mention. I use the delete key a lot.

How much revision went into this poem?

I am constantly revising my work. Even after something is published, I'm still revising.

Is this poem categorical of your work? Why or why not?

Yes. I write free verse and try to tell a story.

What is your favorite line from the poem or the line you are most proud of?

"'Leave the chair,' I yell as he rolls it outside. Dried acrylics adorn the armrests. Blues overlay reds, overlay oranges, overlay greens."

This is the only line that reveals who my daughter was—an artist.

If you had to narrow it down, what three books have had the most impact on your writing?

I have too many favorites. The last book I read informs the next thing I write. I just finished *The Blind Assassin* by Margaret Atwood.

She's a great storyteller. I learned a lot about myself through her insights about humanity, relationships, and people.

Do you work in any other artistic mediums? If so, how do those other genres inform your poetry?

I write creative nonfiction and some fiction. Prose informs my poetry, and poetry informs my prose. I like thinking about words, their multiple meanings, how they sound, how they're perceived.

Based on your personal experience, what advice would you give to other writers?

Read. Read. Read. I'm a novice. For me to say anything more would be presumptuous.

Where can readers find more of your work?

My work has appeared in *The Big Roundtable, Brain, Child Magazine, Hippocampus, Intima,* and in the anthologies *She's Got This: Essays on Standing Strong and Moving On* and *A Cup of Comfort for Parents of Children with Special Needs.*

With Steps or Without

JACOB GRIFFIN HALL

I slide across the back
doorway in a seam-
less light,

an empty
sidestep to revert
beyond myself—

smooth stretch
of timothy or auburn
brushstroke.

My skin, a brushstroke.
My skin, a barrel set out
overnight to collect water.

Each bone recedes
into a fracture,
a picture frame.

The urn hollow
against brick, ridges
of plaster

that leave me
open-handed each time
the season turns.

A backlash of voice
scaling the arch between
shoulder blades

or the bite of a cut
that would govern rather
than let breathe.

A shade tightens over me;
I shiver and feign sleep.

Interview

with Jacob Griffin Hall

What inspired the poem?

This poem grew out of a moment when I caught a glimpse of myself in a mirror. The light through the window by the back door caught the mirror at a funny angle and I just barely caught sight of myself passing through it. This made it so that I registered my reflection for a second but the lines were distorted, blurred. This was less than a year after a friend of mine had passed, and I was still processing that grief. Something about the distorted lines of the self in the mirror seemed to speak to the place I was at emotionally and that ended up being the impulse behind the poem.

What was the hardest part about writing it?

The revision stages. This was one of the poems that I felt was almost right for a long time but there was still something off. I spent two years or so, on and off, going back and tinkering. Eventually it got to a place that I was happy with (though I'm still tempted to go in and adjust an adjective or two).

What came easiest when writing this poem?

The image in the opening tercet was the first thing to come. I've changed the phrasing from first writing, but it's still the same image for the most part.

Was there anything in your original conception that did not make it in?

Yes, a good bit I think. It was a bit more narrative to start and I think six or seven lines longer. It was also originally a bit more excessive with the adjective use.

How much revision went into this poem?

Like I mentioned above, I spent a while tinkering—two years or so. I think most of the major revisions took place within the first month after writing the original draft, though. I was also fortunate enough to be able to workshop the piece with an amazing group of poets, which I'm really thankful for.

Is this poem categorical of your work? Why or why not?

I think this poem fits well with a lot of the poems I was writing at that time. It's been almost four years since I wrote the first draft and the style of my work has shifted a good bit since then. I do think the way this poem treats image and musicality lines up with the other work I was doing around that time.

Who are some of your favorite poets, and what're the three books of poetry you turn to most often?

Mary Ruefle, Adrienne Rich, Robert Hass, Brenda Hillman, Rita Dove, Alice Notley, Natasha Trethewey, Rae Armantrout, Danez Smith—there are so, so many incredible poets. It's hard to pick only a handful.

The three that I turn to the most often, though, are probably Adrienne Rich's *Early Collected Poems*, Mary Ruefle's *Selected Poems*, and Robert Hass' *Sun Under Wood*.

How would you personally define poetry?

Oof. Rebecca Lindenberg said in a *McSweeney's* interview that "you write poems because you have something echoing around in the bone-dome of your skull that you cannot say. Poetry allows us to hold many related tangential notions in very close orbit around each other at the same time." That's one of my favorite takes to share with my students, so I'll go with that.

LATE MAPS (LOBSTER TELEPHONE)

ROB KENAGY

On Television, a man hunts ghosts
in an abandoned prison. Dali believed

space defines us—not time. And the inside
of a skull is a seashell. Just down the sandy path

through the crab grass, the Gulf of Mexico.
Turquoise at once. "Manifest yourself!" the man yells

into an empty cell. A cool Florida current,
tender through our bedroom window.

The screen glow spread on the mattress. Above us,
Orion's belt a kite tail across a grapefruit orchard.

"Manifest and reveal yourself!"
the night-vision image of the man calls out again.

Pearl-tipped tide pools in moonlight,
past the sea wall—past the No Trespassing sign.

"Manifest yourself! Come on out!"
After molting, we're fresh and tangled

in the surf. "Manifest yourself!" Salt-washed.
New tan lines. The palms in our collarbones.

INTERVIEW
WITH ROB KENAGY

What inspired the poem?

A lost weekend on the beach with my partner. We haunted the gulf and hunted cheap souvenir shops—at night we read *The Secret Life of Salvador Dali* out loud. We had a brief moment to escape our working day grind.

What was the hardest part about writing it?

Balancing movement and ideas—I obsess over how images and language work together to help the eye move forward. I constantly rearrange lines to try to chart a clear, thoughtful path through a poem. I worked overtime on this one.

What came easiest when writing this poem?

Being open and available to whatever showed up while writing. That's rarely the case—I often get in my own way, box myself out, and feel clogged up. This poem came from a place I wanted to swim in. I'm grateful I let myself take a dip.

Was there anything in your original concept that did not make it in?

For sure—ten times more ghosts and Dali. And I get goofy on fish, birds, and flowers.

Is there anything unique about your personal writing process?

I put a lot of emphasis on reading. I like to keep a strange range of texts near me at all times. Right now, I'm reading *Sapiens* by Yuval Noah Harari, *Cider* by Annie Proulx and Lew Nichols, *Ripley Under Ground* by Patricia Highsmith, and *& more black* by t'ai freedom ford. I check UFO blogs, NBA news, and the latest shit from the idiot-in-chief. It's an insane buffet that helps me calculate life and language.

Who are some of your favorite poets?

I try not to play favorites. But how 'bout a few artists that inspire me: Elizabeth Bishop, Mary Ruefle, Claudia Rankine, Yoko Ono, Carl Phillips, C.D. Wright, Lou Reed, Rachel B. Glaser, Brenda Hillman, Tanya Olson, Tarfia Faizullah, Matt Hart, Patti Smith, Alice Coltrane, Yo La Tengo, and Homer J. Simpson.

Do you work in any other artistic mediums? If so, how do those other genres inform your poetry?

I'm a musician—communicating through sound helps me leave my body and sink into the cosmos. Making music taps into my indulgent weirdo. I've come to think of this as a strength and weakness.

Poetry forces me to confront the world in words. Using language to make art requires a focused and engaged presence that often feels vulnerable and raw. When I'm working on a poem, I try to face my truths and offer an honest kindness to readers.

I reckon poetry forces me to be a better person.

Based on your personal experience, what advice would you give to other writers?

Embrace the strange and comfort the pain—stay present and open in the universe. Be weird. Be kind.

Enter: Implosion

LAURIN BECKER MACIOS

1.

An imploded person as she appears to a mortician
An imploded person as she appears to the final straw
as she appears to her psychoanalyst

Did your parents implode?
Do you remember witnessing an implosion as a small child?

2.
How to drip with the trappings of yourself ie
What the red/blue states need is

a. poetry
b. jobs
c. my two cents

3.
How to keep your tongue
in the dank cave of your mouth

How to silence by making a show
of your listening

How to listen

0.
How to explode
How to determine in- or ex-

4.
How to recognize your aging face speaking
the foreign tongue of silence

5.
How to expand your new vocabulary

INTERVIEW
WITH LAURIN BECKER MACIOS

How long have you been writing poetry? What has changed from your first poem to your newest work?

Since sixth grade, so that's like twenty-three years? But writing and reading poetry in a more serious way since college, when an Intro to Creative Writing class opened my eyes to contemporary poetry. That's been about sixteen years. My poetry has gotten more quiet, more inspired by landscape, less dramatic to the naked eye.

Who are some of your favorite poets?

Kevin Young and Walt Whitman are up there.

If you had to narrow it down, what three books have had the most impact on your writing?

Sharon Olds' *The Gold Cell* was the first book of contemporary poetry I ever read and it blew the doors open. Whitman's *Leaves of Grass* went everywhere with me for a long time, and that musicality got into my bones. And the Coleman Barks translations of Rumi showed me how breathtaking simplicity can be.

Based on your personal experience, what advice would you give to other writers?

Read poetry!

Where can readers find more of your work?

My chapbook *I Almost was Animal* is available on Amazon, and online poems are linked on my website (laurinbeckermacios.com).

NIGHTJAR

REISER PERKINS

1.

In 1917, Mata Hari blew a kiss to her firing squad. Afterwards, they sealed her head in a jar of formaldehyde for exhibition at a Paris museum. Sometime before the advent of television, interest waned in the exotic dancer / alleged spy and the head was put in storage.

Red hair floating like slow serpents in murky green, alone for decades and unseen until some heart-bent docent goes searching through the dim stacks, in love with the idea of things and finding, at last, the row and the shelf. See as he sees the dusty spot where the jar once was but is no longer. The twice stolen head.

Just because something's gone doesn't mean it doesn't still exist in the known world, which is made by us, as is the entire horrendous future and even God who only wants us to finally see the garden and die.

Meanwhile, a video of a man dressed like a dinosaur while riding a horse makes the rounds, as if to say: discover small things to be a warrior about. The whole thing makes you proud to be an animal, hidden, self-generated. Now take that feeling and bury it up to the neck. Plant it so it may grow into something that embraces whatever. Remember, the head is not a sanctuary, only a stupid yawning thing, and trapped.

2.

The Yazidi believe that Adam and Eve quarreled over who could create a person without the help of the other person. To see who was right, they each stored their seed in a jar. The jars were then buried and forgotten for a long time during which Adam and Eve went on with their lives, bathing in spring fed streams and giving names to all the animals.

Then one day they remembered their argument and dug up the jars. Eve's was emitting an eerie light and a sound like music, only they didn't know about music so it freaked them out a little. When Eve opened her jar, many bugs and snakes crawled out, plus a couple of mice.

Adam was terrified of all these things so he screamed and ran around in little circles while waving his hands around. Eve stood and calmly replaced the jar's lid, stepping on a centipede with her bare foot. Finally, Adam calmed down enough to open his own jar. Inside was a beautiful boy child. He named him Son of Jar.

As a boy, Son of Jar was unable to step outside of a line traced around him in the dirt. All of Mesopotamia was his playground, but he couldn't tell sky from sand. His heart was in his eyeball, the old women used to say. His only interest was perfection, which didn't exist. When he grew up, he married a beautiful virgin. She didn't exist either.

3.

"My mama wants to be pickled and put in a jar when she dies," said someone in a grocery store in 2003.

The wind had been howling for days. It sounded far away but then would suddenly remind us about itself by rattling windows, knocking over vases. A creature inhabited the roof. At night, while we dreamt of being re-educated in an underground city, it would thump and root.

Then we dreamt we were in Texas. Our rental car had come with a dead body in the trunk. Were they trying to frame us? It was the corpse of a traveling salesman. Did he drink himself to death? Was he murdered? It seemed our only option was to dump the body, but where? We couldn't find a single river or tree and the dry ground was hard. Even though we were really stressed out and were about to miss our flight, we were getting along exceptionally well.

During the day, we were content and therefor didn't accomplish much. We planted a couple of dahlias, took a shower, talked to Poncho, checked the mail. In the kitchen, the dishwasher did its thing. Little awkwardnesses were arrayed like ducks around the old people. So this was what it meant to live in awe of silence and the basic brain's pedestrian clarity.

INTERVIEW

WITH REISER PERKINS

What inspired the poem?

"Nightjar" was inspired by 1) seeing a headline that Mata Hari's head had been stolen from a museum 2) learning about the Yazidi, a group that today lives mostly in Iraq but whose religious beliefs can be traced back to ancient Mesopotamia and 3) overhearing something someone said in a grocery store. Not necessarily in that order. These three (let's call them) occasions are connected by one thing and one thing only—jars—but it took me years to notice that and put them together. Before that, they existed as separate poems, each lacking an axis. Now they spin around each other in a way I hope is as satisfying to the reader as it somehow is to me.

Was there anything in your original concept that did not make it in?

Oh plenty. I struggled to find a way to include Mata Hari's last words which were, "Harlot, yes. Traitoress, never." I put them in and took them out and put them back in over a dozen times at least. I'm still not sure they shouldn't be in there.

How much revision went into this poem?

I revise everything I do ad nauseam. This poem was no different. I'd look at it every few months for years, starting about fifteen years ago. I'm not even kidding. If not for this miraculous publication, I'm sure I'd still be writing it.

Is this poem categorical of your work? Why or why not?

Yes. There's a certain willingness or openness and a skewed sensibility here that I think makes its way into almost everything I write. I love reading and writing prose poems, but my attempts are not usually well received. This is only the second such piece to be "accepted."

How long have you been writing poetry? What has changed from your first poem to your newest work?

I wrote my first poem when I was about nine or ten, which was approximately thirty or so years ago. That first poem was about a black dog standing in the road. It was called "Black Dog" and was weird and mournful, so nothing has really changed I guess.

Who are some of your favorite poets?

Laurie Anderson, Federico Garcia Lorca, Robert Duncan, Charles Simic, and WS Merwin.

Do you work in any other artistic mediums? If so, how do those other genres inform your poetry?

I'm a musician. Writing songs has helped me understand why simplicity is good. My trajectory as a writer has been from the baroque to what I'd like to think is a kind of psychedelic minimalism.

How would you personally define poetry?

I just always stick to what Wallace Stevens famously said: "The poem is the cry of its occasion."

Based on your personal experience, what advice would you give to other writers?

Read everything all of the time. And don't be a snob about it. Authentic curiosity is the cure for what ails the species.

Where can readers find more of your work?

Tin House, Hobart, and most recently *New State Review.*

Topography of a Wound

Helli Fang

I'll only say this once. My mother pinches
the seams of pork dumplings
as if she is afraid to hear them speak. My father spits out
pig feet bones like they are bullets.
In a Chinatown alley,
a skeleton falls to its knees inside its flesh
& shivers
like a wind-up toy in a plastic bag—

The last time I knelt for a man
was in an Applebee's parking lot. I cut a slit
in his belly, ate the guts & bones, and
placed a phoenix inside
just to see if it would fit.
When I visit my ancestors' graves
I leave a bouquet of trout spines
instead of lilies.

My mother's cabbage leaves
know how to choose their own colors
in the rain: the sobs of lightning
forcing us to look up at the sky. My mother
pinches the seams of pork dumplings
as if she is growing a garden of bruises.

& that night,
we stuck our hairdryers out the window
like silvered snipers
to try and talk back to the wind. How
the moonlight burned our flesh bright blue.
How we turned off all the lights in the house
& fell to our knees
just to hear the sound of bone.

INTERVIEW

WITH HELLI FANG

What inspired the poem?

This poem came from a prompt from a poetry workshop I was taking, where we were asked to write a poem based on Michael Palmer's "Musica Ficta." That poem is full of mysterious contradictions—the speaker's voice constantly circles around itself, repeating lines such as "I will tell you a story" and "I will speak of this" in spite of its powerful opening line: "This I will never tell." I loved how assertive the poem is despite it being completely contradictory, as it feels almost like the speaker is letting the reader in on something secret, something vulnerable. I wanted to create a similar effect in my own poem by opening with the line "I'll only say this once," yet at the same time filling the poem's space with recurring images, words, and themes.

What was the hardest part about writing it?

I feel this about all my poems, but this one especially, that it is really difficult to be truthful in my work. I am often honest, but not truthful—meaning that I tend not to tell genuine, real-life events in my works, instead leaning towards imagined stories or mythologies. With this poem's opening line—"I'll only say this once"—I felt that this poem would be much more powerful if it held some sense of truth within it, so I began it with an incredibly familiar image to me: my mother making dumplings in the kitchen. I felt that by giving up a truth in this poem, I could build towards that same kind of intimately confessional voice that Palmer's poem also carried.

Is there anything unique about your personal writing process?

I'm not sure if this is necessarily unique, but I like to actively read at the same time I am writing. I usually have some of my favorite poetry books beside me, and I pick them up and skim through words that might spark something in me to form sentences and images. I also cry a lot when I write, sometimes on purpose. I just do everything I possibly can to stir up enough emotions inside of me to write something I feel that I need to write.

How long do you usually spend working on a single poem?

I usually can write the first draft of a poem within four to five hours, often in one sitting. The revision process takes much longer, though, usually spanning over several weeks. I like to put the poem away for some time after I write it, so I can read it again with a fresh pair of eyes and work out what needs to be changed.

Who are some of your favorite poets?

Ocean Vuong, Eduardo C. Corral, Richard Siken, Li-Young Lee, Kristin Chang, Solmaz Sharif, Adrienne Rich, among many others.

Do you work in any other artistic mediums? If so, how do those other genres inform your poetry?

I've played violin for over twelve years, and I find that playing music has trained my ears to grow an instinct to sound. I like to revise my poems by reciting them out loud, tweaking words and images based on how the language both sounds to my ears and feels in my mouth. I think it's very much like sitting in a practice room, playing a small section of a piece over and over again until it sounds right under my fingers.

Where can readers find more of your work?

My poem "Obituary in Red Envelope" was very recently published in *The Margins* (Asian American Writer's Workshop). You can also read some newer works of mine in *Salt Hill*, *Columbia Journal*, and *DIALOGIST*!

“ANOTHER ME INSIDE OF ME” | YASUAKI OKAMOTO

"IN THE CLOUDS" | JANESSA MULEPATI

PROLOGUE

By Nick Francis Potter

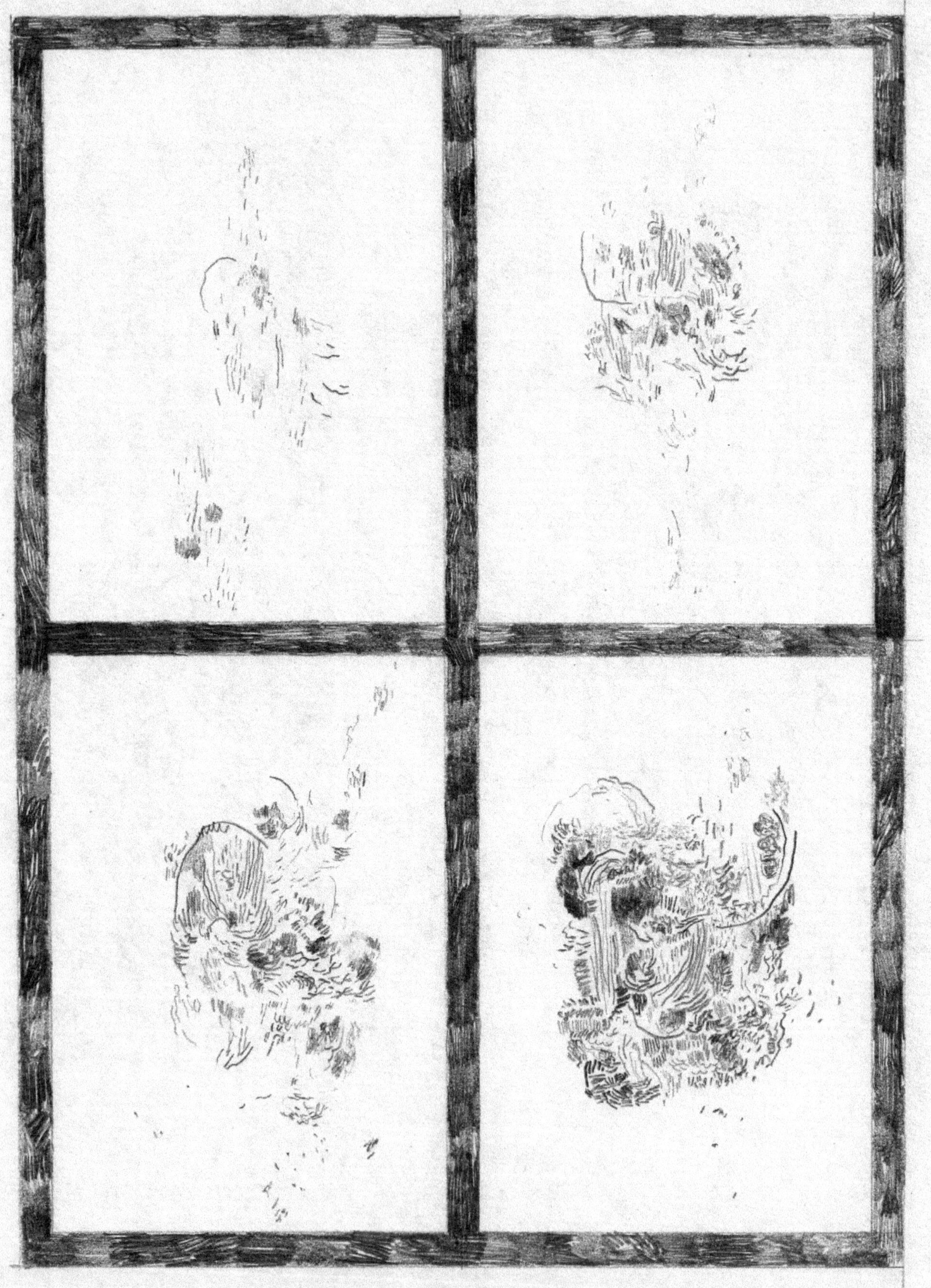

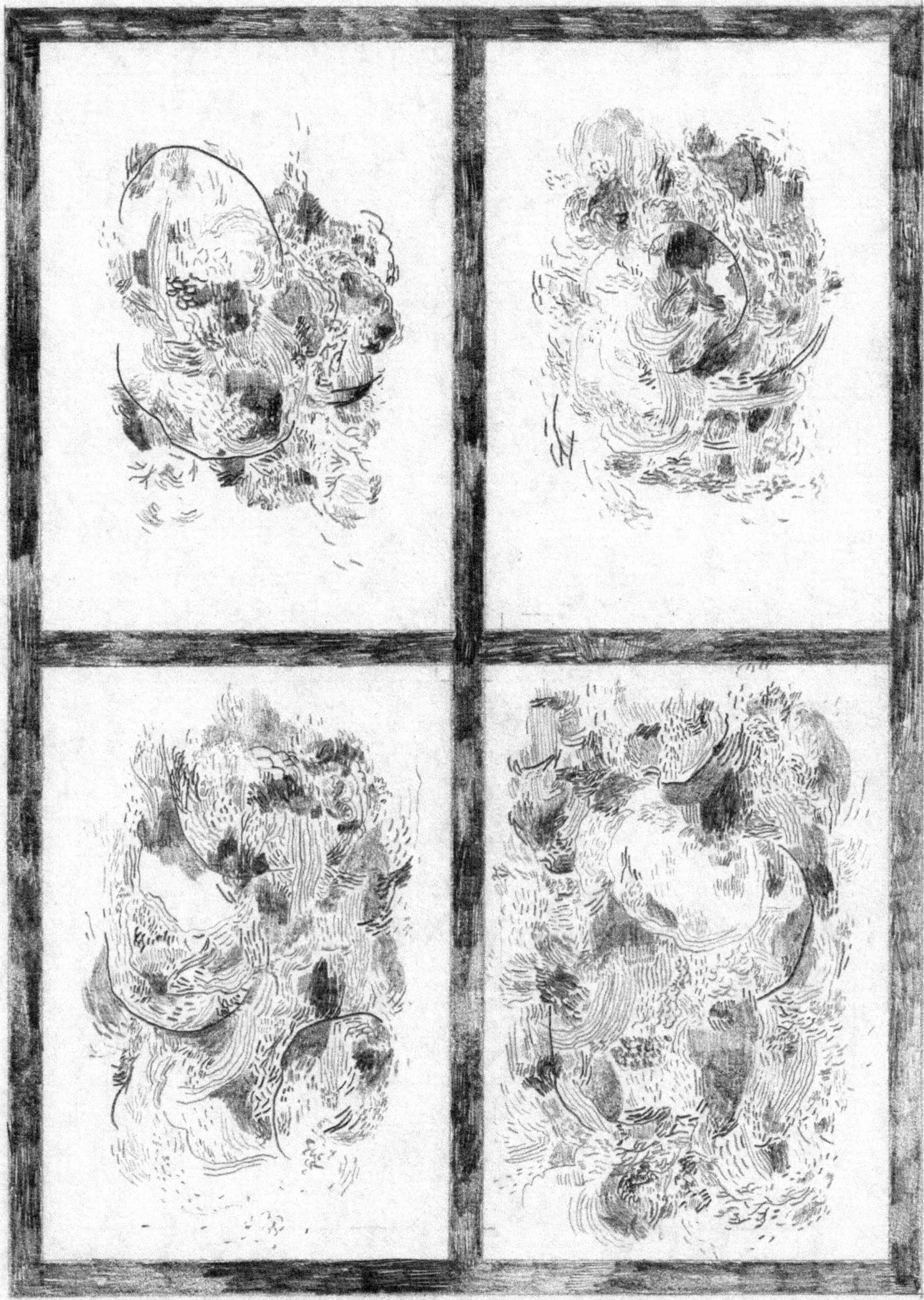

INTERVIEW
WITH NICK FRANCIS POTTER

This work is admittedly and wonderfully abstract. Does your writing process change when working on more abstract comics?

If we're considering cartooning a form of writing, which I do, then yes, wholesale abstraction, like what you see in "Prologue," definitely alters the process. Drawing out the linguistic analogy, it's probably most closely related to the practice of automatic writing, but even that doesn't feel totally accurate. In truth, when I've abandoned semantic meaning, it turns into something more instinctive and primal, with lots of improvisation—more akin to music, like jazz. Having said that, I have created a lot of comics that couple abstract images with language, and in those instances, the writing also changes: the material qualities of the language become heightened, and the semantic meaning begins to breakdown and abstract, in concert with the art.

More to that point, do you find there is a different intention behind creating abstract work?

Absolutely. It often feels more personal, corporeal even, in nature. What I'm capturing in the marks is a sense of motion—the fluidity of my body connecting the instrument, whatever it is, to the paper or canvas. It's a kind of meditative practice, a state of mindlessness, not unrelated to some forms of non-competitive athletic activity, I think. And so, if I'm trying to derive meaning from it, it comes after the fact. In the moment, the intention is mark-making, in all its gravity and simplicity.

Tell us a little more about the drafting process. What was the hardest part of crafting this comic?

The comic started out of a satisfaction with a few marks I was playing with, and some of the variations that I stumbled upon in the first panel. The difficulty, then, was to create some continuity between panels, and maintain a visual relationship from panel to panel, that maintained that. That might sound obvious, but it's difficult, sometimes, to maintain patterns, including the weight and contrast of the marks made, while also surprising yourself in the process. And, with this particular series, it's rather laborious. So, the four pages were basically me running through the number of variations I could come up with, combined with my stamina for making the thing, and keeping interested.

What instruments did you use here?

Pencil. I made it all with a mechanical pencil with 0.9 diameter lead.

Besides pencil, what other comic mediums do you work in? Do you have a particular preference?

I like to experiment widely. It's part of the joy and discovery in making comics. So I've worked with various pencils, chalks, ink, and pens, in addition to watercolor paint, acrylic, silkscreen printing, and collage from old magazines. On occasion I've colored my work digitally, but generally I keep things analog, mostly out of convenience. At my core, though, I think I'm most attached to the pencil. I like the subtle range of penciling, including the messiness of smudges and erasure. I've always been drawn to the transparency and malleability of pencil on the page.

Transitioning from creating artwork to fully-fledged comics can often feel daunting for artists. Do you have any tips for aspiring comic writers? What were things you wish you would have known when you were starting out?

I wanted to make comics ever since I was a kid, but it wasn't until I took a deep dive into independent comics that I realized the range of what was possible in the form, and that's what gave me motivation. I was reading Don Hertzfeldt and Dina Kelberman, who were making brilliant comics with glorified stick figures, and it was only then that I realized, I can do this. And it was only when I just tried making comics that things changed. So, if I had any advice to give to someone who wants to make comics, it's this: (1) read as many different kinds of comics as you can get your hands on, and (2) give yourself a short term goal, and try making a comic. Once you start it'll be hard to stop.

These pages are a part of a much longer work, correct?

Yes. This is, aptly, the prologue to a collection of comics from a manuscript titled *Big Gorgeous Jazz Machine*. The collection contains a range of experiments with the comics form, including abstract comics and comics poetry.

When we were talking through publishing this piece, we asked if you wanted to go untitled or with this original title. You said it was up to the editors. "Prologue" seems an origin story, even when viewed as separate from the larger work to which it belongs: it begins with almost nothing, expands, then shrinks into itself. Even excerpted, the title "Prologue" is apt. Would you consider this an origin story? What do you make of the arc of the piece?

I definitely think there is something embryonic about the piece—a kind of molecular coming together. It's true, too, that while the creation of the piece lacked a specific narrative intention, or a desire for representation, I've begun to think about it in those terms after the fact. I think the drawing in last panel, for instance, kind of resembles a heart, and so the expansion and contraction prior to that panel has taken on a kind of slow-motion heartbeat, or an abstracted breath. The practice of abstraction feels, sometimes, like a kind of warm-up—an activity to just get your hands moving and making marks—and it's something of a surprise where you end up. It reasserts the sense of discovery of what you're doing in the act of doing it, which I think is important to any artistic endeavor.

If you had to narrow it down, who would you say are your three biggest influences?

This is really a wicked question, I think. There are undoubtedly hundreds, maybe thousands. But, if I'm focusing on comics, and not thinking too hard about it, I'd say Renée French's *h day*, Warren Craghead's *How to be Everywhere*, and Aidan Koch's *After Nothing Comes*. And sorry, one more: Jason Overby's *The Being Being*.

What other mediums have influenced your work? How?

Music, modern and contemporary art, literary fiction and poetry, film, television, video games, architecture, web design—you name it. I become easily enamored, I suppose, and have a tendency to want to do everything, so I try to fold as many of my interests into each other as possible, when I can. A recent example of this is my series of comics called "Static Gifs for Broken Musicians". The series is a collection of single-page abstract comics that are inspired by contemporary musicians (like Bill Orcutt, Okkyung Lee, and Matana Robert) who are creating innovative and, for lack of a better word, difficult music. I've always been interested in visual representations of sound, and I thought that comics, since they lend themselves to the illusion of movement and time by their sequential structure, would be a unique way to approach this interest. And because I was creating homages to abstract musicians, inevitably, the comics were also inspired by abstract expressionists like Joan Mitchell and Cy Twombly. And because I also included language—specifically the HTML code for gifs—I was thinking, too, about concrete poetry, with nods to pioneering poets like Apollinaire & Kenneth Patchen.

Where can our readers find more of your work? Have you been published before?

I have collection of short stories, comics, and hybrid stories titled *New Animals*, from *Subito Press*. More recently, I have published comics in *The Offing*, *Quarterly West*, *Big Other*, *TYPO Magazine*, *Heavy Feather Review*, and *Entropy*.

What are your own artistic goals for the future? Simply, what do you want to do next?

I have a few pokers in the fire: I'm working on a biographical comic with my wife and partner, Erin, about Eliza Partridge, and her sister Emily, nineteenth century pioneers and members of the early Mormon church during their practice of polygamy. I'm also working a middle-grade novel about a young girl who grows a beard and becomes a pirate. There are some other odds and ends, but these two are the most prominent.

CONTRIBUTORS

ALAN SINCIC earned his MFA at Western New England University and Columbia, served on the editorial board of the *Columbia Review*, and—back in the day—published a children's chapter book, *Edward Is Only A Fish* (*Henry Holt*) that was reviewed in the *New York Times*, translated into German, and recently issued in a Kindle edition. His novella *The Babe* won the 2014 Knickerbocker Prize from *Big Fiction Magazine*, the short story/performance piece "Sugar" aired on Seattle's Hollow Earth Radio, the short story "Random Sample" is currently available online in the Prize Winner's Issue of *Hunger Mountain Journal* (hungermtn.org), and the short story "Sand" appeared in *The Greensboro Review.* The short story "The Deluge" appeared in the *New Ohio Review* and "The Hunting Of The Famous People" won *The Gateway Review* 2019 Flash Fiction Contest. *A3 Press* published a unique (fold-out map style) illustrated chapbook of *My New Car.*

MEGAN SWENSON is a fiction writer from Chandler, Arizona. She received her MFA from New York University and has since been living in Vancouver, British Columbia with her husband. An excerpt from her novel-in-progress, *Before This We Are Nothing*, was shortlisted for the Stockholm Writers Festival First Pages Prize in 2018.

NICOLE ZDEB is a writer based in Portland, OR. She holds a MFA from Iowa Writers' Workshop. In 2011 *Bedouin Press* published her chapbook, *The Friction of Distance.*

MATTHEW RICKART was born in New England and lives in Chicago. His writing has been published in *The Madison Review, Short Fiction Break, Danse Macabre,* and *Plain China.* He is always at work on a novel.

ANNIE CIGIC hails from Cleveland, Ohio. Her work has appeared or is forthcoming in *The Bookends Review, Gordon Square Review, honey & lime, Havik*, and elsewhere. She holds an MFA in poetry from Bowling Green State University and is a first-year PhD candidate in Rhetoric and Writing.

JIWON CHOI is a poet, teacher, and urban gardener. She teaches preschool at the Educational Alliance, a multi-generation non-profit located on the Lower East Side of NYC. She is also a long-time urban gardener and membership coordinator for the Pacific Street Brooklyn Bear's Community Garden located near Downtown Brooklyn. *One Daughter is Worth Ten Sons,* published by *Hanging Loose Press* in 2017, is her first book of poetry. She lives in Brooklyn, NY.

KATHLEEN RADIGAN hails from rural Rhode Island. She holds a BA from Wesleyan University and an MFA from Boston University. Her poems have been published by *The Academy of American Poets, PANK Blog, Carve, The New Ohio Review*, and a few other places. She lives in Brooklyn, where she babysits and teaches English to gifted high-school students. She is a Fall 2019 Brooklyn Poets Fellow.

SAM STOKLEY is a disabled artist and educator from Peoria, IL living in Minneapolis. A finalist for the 2019 *BOAAT* Chapbook Prize, his writing is found in *Fairy Tale Review, Poetry City, Brevity,* and other homes. His essay, "How to Discuss Race as a White Person," was selected for a Best of *Brevity* anthology, due out in Fall

2020 from *Rose Metal Press* (eds. Zoë Bossiere, Dinty W. Moore). Sam has recessive dystrophic epidermolysis bullosa. Find him on Instagram (@bovinii).

TAYLOR IMEL is a writer from Roanoke. She holds a BA in Nonfiction Writing from Columbia College in Chicago, where she currently resides alongside Cesar and Frankie. Big thank you to all who hugged her last year. She's assembling a new work on concepts of photographs and inheritance. Stay kind and stay tuned online (taylorkimel.wordpress.com) or follow her on Instagram (@tayimel).

DANIEL ARISTI was born in Spain. He studied French Literature as an undergrad (French Lycée in San Sebastian). He now lives and writes in Brussels. Daniel's work is forthcoming or has been recently featured in *Dewpoint, decomP, Temenos Journal,* and *Main Street Rag.*

HARRIET HEYDEMANN is an MFA candidate in the Creative Writing Program at San Francisco State University. Her work has appeared in *The Big Roundtable, Brain, Child Magazine, Hippocampus,* and in the anthologies, *A Cup of Comfort for Children with Special Needs* and in *She's Got This: Essays on Standing Strong and Moving On.* She lives near San Francisco with her husband, Gary, and their dog, Rico.

JACOB GRIFFIN HALL is from Atlanta, GA. He is currently a PhD student in English at the University of Missouri. His work has appeared or is forthcoming in *New South, The Carolina Quarterly, Poetry South, Madcap Review, Santa Ana River Review, Stirring, Menacing Hedge,* and other journals.

ROB KENAGY is an artist and writer based in New York City. His work has appeared in zines, journals, and other strange places. He's a member of the multi-disciplinary collaborative BIG LOTTO and makes music as Ganges. Rob earned an MFA from Virginia Tech and teaches free community writing courses.

LAURIN BECKER MACIOS is the author of *Somewhere to Go*, winner of the 19th annual Poetry Award from *Elixir Press*, and *I Almost Was Animal*, winner of the 2018 *Writer's Relief* WaterSedge Poetry Chapbook Prize. She lives in New York City with her husband, son, and French Bulldog. You can find her online (laurinbeckermacios.com).

REISER PERKINS' work can be found in *Tin House, Hobart,* and elsewhere. A former journalist based in Cairo, Egypt, she currently resides on the island of Maui where she works for The Merwin Conservancy, a non-profit founded by W.S. Merwin. She also edits the digital magazine *Otis Nebula.* You can find her online (www.reiserperkins.com).

HELLI FANG is an undergraduate student at Bard College. Her poetry has appeared or is forthcoming in *The Margins, Salt Hill Journal, The Adroit Journal, DIALOGIST, Blueshift Journal, Columbia Journal, Alexandria Quarterly, Wildness,* and more, and she's been recognized by the Scholastic Art & Writing Awards, Columbia College of Chicago, and Bennington College. She has also participated in programs such as the Iowa Young Writer's Workshop, The Adroit Mentorship Program, and The Speakeasy Project. When Helli is not writing, she enjoys playing the violin and climbing trees.

COZ FRIMPONG is a muddy watercolor illustrator based in New Jersey. You can keep up with the mess on instagram (@evzosart).

JANELLE CORDERO is an interdisciplinary artist and educator living in the seventh most hipster city in the U.S. Both her writing and her paintings are sparse narratives that emphasize the disconnected nature of the human condition. Her writing has been published in dozens of literary journals, including *Harpur Palate* and *The Louisville Review*, while her paintings have been featured in venues throughout the Pacific Northwest. Janelle has authored two full-length poetry collections and two chapbooks. Her latest collection, *Woke to Birds*, was released in October 2019. Stay connected with Janelle's work online (www.janellecordero.com).

YASUAKI OKAMOTO is a NY based Japanese artist

who lived in England, Spain, and Canada. Yasuaki studied at The Art Students League of New York and The National Academy Museum and School. He is a recipient of a Yasuo Kuniyoshi Award 2018 for Printmaking, Edward G. McDowell Travel Grant 2014, Xavier Gonzalez and Ethel Edwards Travel Grant 2013, Lawrence Littman Scholarship 2012, Mary Birmingham Award 2010, and more. He has exhibited about hundred shows mainly in New York City, including The Affordable Art Fair NYC, National Academy Museum, Corey Helford Gallery, Art Expo NY, Spectrum Miami, Agora Gallery, and The Art Revolution Taipei. He held a solo exhibition at the Sasebo City Museum Shimanose Art Center in August 2018. Also, his work appears in art magazine, newspaper, and many public and private collections, notably The Sylvia Wald and Po Kim Art Gallery New York, The Williamsburg Art Historical Center, and more.

JANESSA MULEPATI lives in the northeast United States. She is a writer and artist, and in all of her creative pursuits, hopes to capture the viewer's imagination—to whisper in their ear that something big is unfolding. She believes that art, at its best, reminds us that every single person has a rich life, inner and outer, that we will barely come to know. Find her on Instagram (@nessi.writes).

NICK FRANCIS POTTER is a writer, cartoonist, and educator living in Columbia, Missouri. He is the author of *New Animals*, winner of the *Subito Press* Prize for Innovative Prose, published in 2016. His prose and comics have been featured in *Ninth Letter, Black Warrior Review, Sleepingfish, Caketrain, Fourteen Hills, The Chattahoochee Review,* and *The Los Angeles Review of Books*, among many others. He is the comics editor for *ANMLY* (formerly *Drunken Boat*). He has an MFA from Brown University and a PhD in English from the University of Missouri, where he currently teaches writing and theory in the Digital Storytelling Program.

www.ingramcontent.com/pod-product-compliance
Lightning Source LLC
Chambersburg PA
CBHW082123180726
48291CB00011B/2818

* 9 7 8 1 9 4 9 0 6 5 0 5 3 *